American ME

Teens Write About the Immigrant Experience

By Youth Communication

Edited by Marie Glancy O'Shea

True Stories by Teens

American ME

EXECUTIVE EDITORS
Keith Hefner and Laura Longhine

CONTRIBUTING EDITORS
Philip Kay, Hope Vanderberg, Clarence Haynes, Katia Hetter,
Rachel Blustain, Duffy Cohen, Al Desetta, Nora McCarthy,
Andrea Estepa, Tamar Rothenberg, and Duffie Cohen

LAYOUT & DESIGN
Efrain Reyes, Jr. and Jeff Faerber

PRODUCTION
Stephanie Liu

COVER ART
YC Art Dept.

ISBN 978-1-935552-48-2

Second, Expanded Edition

Printed in the United States of America

Youth Communication ®
New York, New York
www.youthcomm.org

Catalog Item #YD03-1

Dedication

To the New York City International High Schools. More than 75 students from the International High Schools have held writing internships at Youth Communication. Many of their stories are in this book.

Includes stories by teens from:

Albania
Bangladesh,
Brazil
China
Dominican Republic
Ecuador
El Salvador
Ghana
Haiti
India
Iran
Iraq
Korea
Malaysia
Mexico
Philippines
Peru
Russia
Senegal
Venezuela
Yemen

Table of Contents

Contents

When I Learned English I Found My Voice

*At a high school for immigrants, Sandra feels
comfortable enough to master English.*

Putting My Foot Down in a Place I Call Home

*Growing up in Venezuela, Francis moves with her
mother to four different cities and switches schools
eight times. In the U.S., Francis finally puts her foot
down.*

Using the Book

Introduction

In this book, teens who have moved to the United States from around the world describe the experience of adjusting to a new country and a new life. They examine the feelings that come with such a significant transition, from excitement and pride to nervousness and frustration. "Fitting in" takes on a whole new meaning for adolescents in this situation; they are often torn between sharing in the American culture of their peers and remaining connected to their families' traditions. In these pages they discuss that conflict, their loneliness and longing for the familiar, and their discoveries of new food, new friends, and a new identity.

Immigration is disorienting. Often it strains family bonds by introducing distance and distrust. Edwidge Danticat describes the bewilderment she faces on arriving in the U.S. from Haiti at age 12 to live for the first time with her immediate family. Her mother hugs her in joy, but Edwidge—who hadn't even remembered what her parents looked like—feels "like an orphan being adopted against her will." And while America is a place most immigrant teens know from TV and movies, life rarely mirrors art—especially for those whose families uphold the customs and culture of their homelands. "When I arrived I had great hope for my new life in America," writes Yuh-Yng Lee. "All I wanted was to be a typical American kid with a typical American family." But her parents remain exacting and emotionally reserved, unlike the parents who hug and encourage their children on popular sit-coms.

Writers in this book find ways to deal with the gap between American dreams and their own American realities. Mohammad Hussain learns to value his parents' protectiveness, and Raquel Fernandes finds adversity has helped her grow up. In "American at Heart—But Not on Paper," an anonymous writer goes about making a living as an undocumented immigrant and declares,

"My desire is to contribute to society and help my community prosper, and in this sense I don't need to be a citizen to be a good American." Anna Jakimiuk-Chu, meanwhile, volunteers to gather signatures in support of the DREAM Act to help undocumented teens move toward citizenship. She's inspired by the cause because her ideal America is "a place where everyone deserves a chance to follow their dreams, and in turn to make America a better place for everyone else who has a dream."

Of course, the changes that come with moving to America can throw old dreams and expectations into question. Once content to marry young and forego college, Orubba Almansouri develops a passion for education, and a dread that her father will choose to cut hers short. Zeena Bhattacharya learns to see her parents' violence toward her as abuse, and decides stand up for herself and other children in the same situation.

Often, though, the biggest struggle for newly arrived teens is simply missing people and things left behind—from godparents to goats, markets to moon festivals. Recognizing the benefits of living in America doesn't save immigrant teens from bouts of nostalgia and loneliness. Agelta Arqimandriti remembers the horrors of her old life, but also the friends who made her happy. After visiting her poor but tight-knit relatives in the Philippines, Leneli Liggayu is no longer sure that she, living in America, has the better deal: "I'd miss their food, laughter, and love."

But even as they're torn between two places, these teens know that in their American lives, fitting in means reaching out. Aissata Kebe marvels at the misconceptions her new classmates have about her home continent, and decides to set the record straight. Philippe Sainvil recounts how his fractured soccer team came together across boundaries of nationality. When she lets her guard down and makes friends, Francis Madi finally feels at home.

For all these teens, immigration is a pivotal life experience. It's a bigger and more consequential change than most people their age ever face, but it teaches them about themselves and about the world. Whether through the achievement of becoming fluent in English, the anxiety of seeing their parents struggle, or the exhilaration of discovering they can shape their own futures, teens emerge from the immigrant experience as different people. These stories will help both foreign and native-born teens to better understand the triumphs, tolls, and above all, contradictions that go along with that transformation.

Chapter 1:
Arrival

Jean Sassine

A New World Full of Strangers

By Edwidge Danticat

I could hear nothing over the deafening engine of the airplane, but I certainly could see their faces. They waved goodbye wildly, as though this was a happy occasion. They seemed so thrilled that I was finally going off to the rich and prosperous city of New York. I was sad beyond the limits of my 12 years of life.

One of the stewardesses grabbed me from the doorway and quickly led me inside. Their waves. . . their smiles. . . their cheers were no more. I solemnly followed her to the seat I was to take. She flashed her smile and I was left alone for the trip.

The tears that I fought so bravely before fell uncontrollably into my lap. I was leaving my aunt, uncle, and countless cousins to embark on a mysterious trip to be with parents I barely knew and brothers I'd never met.

The stewardess woke me when the plane landed. Before I

knew what was happening, she and I were filing down an end-less tunnel toward what seemed like a crowd of caretakers.

First the people who made ID cards pulled me aside and snapped my picture. Then the people who handled the bags rushed me through a line to grab my suitcase. Soon, ahead of the other passengers, I was out of the airport.

Since I did not remember what my parents looked like, I was very frightened when a tall, bearded man started to hug me. I was even more afraid when a chubby woman placed her arms around me and exclaimed, "At last my little girl is home!" I felt like an orphan who was being adopted against her will.

The ride home was no more comforting than the meeting with my parents. I was squashed between my three brothers in the back seat of the car while my parents and uncle were crowd-ed in the front seat. My American brothers, who had given me timid hugs before piling into the car, were now curiously staring at me. I imagined they were as anxious to know where I'd come from as I was to know where I was going.

Perhaps if they had asked me who I was, I would have explained that it was not my fault at all that I was entering their lives. To feed and clothe our family, my parents had to desert me so early in life that now I did not even know them. The boys had probably heard about the problems in Haiti: the poverty, the oppression, the despair. I wanted to plead with them to accept me, not stare at me. But I suddenly realized that they had every right to stare. I was, after all, a stranger—even to my own family.

To avoid their glares, I turned to the car window. There must have been hundreds of thousands of lights speeding by. I tried to imagine how much money it had taken to bathe the city in such brightness. God, I thought, this must be the richest country on the planet.

Our home was a great disappointment. It was on the sixth floor of a graffiti-covered building. In Haiti, homes were almost always open and spotless. In my new building, the doors were shut and dusty. When we reached the two-bedroom apartment my family lived in, I hesitated before going inside. The door looked like a cage. When my father fastened the filthy lock, I felt like I was in prison.

My parents did not wait long to enroll me in school. I could barely tell the difference between "hi" and "high" before I found myself in the car heading for Intermediate School 320. The school building had even more graffiti than our apartment building.

In Haiti, schools and churches were treated with utmost

I suddenly realized that they had every right to stare. I was a stranger—even to my own family.

respect. Here things were obviously not the same. I wanted to run back to the car as my father and I walked by a crowd of students laughing hysterically. In my pink cotton dress and yellow sneakers, I was sure they were laughing at me.

As we entered the building, I held my father's hand so tightly one would have thought that my life depended on it. In my school back home, I had been the best memorizer and the most articulate student. I had never given any teacher reason to hit me. Here I was sure that I would fail no matter how hard I tried.

Fortunately, there was a Haitian gentleman in the office. He had a brief talk with my father and made him sign some papers. Then the gentleman walked me to my homeroom class. As I left my father and fought my way past the shoves of the hurried students in the halls, I felt as though I had been abandoned once again.

The Haitian gentleman introduced me to the homeroom teacher and then to one of the many Haitian girls in the class. He told me that she was one of the most respected girls in the school, mostly because of her roughness. The first day, my new friend kindly escorted me from class to class and made me sit next to her in every one.

Despite her help, I could not understand what was being said around me. As far as I was concerned, the teachers might as well have been hitting spoons against the blackboards. I understood nothing. The classes all blended into one long, discouraging day. To make things worse, each time I stepped into the halls the thought of being abused by the other students scared me.

My fear was not realized until the last period, when our class ate lunch. One of the girls on the lunch line lifted my skirt up in the air and began to laugh. During her fit of laughter, she managed to spit out the word "Haitian" as though it were the filthiest and funniest word she'd ever said in her entire life.

Because my new friend intervened, my humiliation that day was brief. After everyone found out that I was always with her, no one tried to touch me again. But unfortunately, the verbal abuse did not stop. "Haitians are filthy. They have AIDS. They stink." Even when I could not understand the actual words, the hatred with which they were expressed hurt me deeply.

She spat out the word "Haitian" as though it were the filthiest and funniest word she'd ever said in her entire life.

Now that I've grown to understand every insult, they hurt even more. In the same way that my brothers glared at me my first day in this country, people often glare at me as though searching for some sign of my nationality. If I don't fit their particular stereotype, they challenge me. They ask me whether I am sure that I am really Haitian.

Being any kind of immigrant isn't easy. Nevertheless, the view of Haitian immigrants has made us ashamed among our peers. The boat people and those few stricken with AIDS have served as profiles for all of us.

If only those who abuse us would ask, perhaps we'd explain that it is not our fault that we are intruding on their existence. To avoid brutal deaths and lead better lives, we are forced to leave our homes.

We'd plead with them to accept us and accommodate us, not make life miserable for us. Because, yes, we are strangers. Unfortunate strangers in a world full of strangers.

Edwidge was 18 when she wrote this story. She went on to graduate from Barnard College, earn an MFA from Brown University, and publish several acclaimed fiction and nonfiction books, including Breath, Eyes, Memory *(1994) and* Brother, I'm Dying *(2007).*

More Than Lions and Poverty

By Aissata Kebe

"Do you raise lions and monkeys as pets in Africa?"

When a boy in my 11th grade English class asked me that question, I was so angry and surprised that I didn't know what to say. Why would someone ask such a silly question about my beautiful continent? I told him that I'd only seen lions and monkeys when I went to the zoo with my family.

I'm from Dakar, the capital city of Senegal, a country in West Africa. The only animals we raise as pets are cats and dogs. Some people like to raise chickens, and in the smaller villages in the country, some raise cows and sheep. Lions and monkeys only live in the wild, and wild lions are rare in West Africa.

It hurts to know that so many people are clueless about Africa. I'm especially disappointed that my classmates—most of whom are also immigrants—have ignorant ideas about the continent. Africa isn't just the images of wild animals and poor or sick people you see on TV. It's a beautiful continent, with 53 countries and hundreds of different languages.

Luckily, I wasn't the only African student in my class at Brooklyn International High School. My friend Tidiane is from Guinea in West Africa, and he told me not to bother answering stupid questions. He said sometimes he answers by making up scary things about Africa, saying it's all one big jungle with elephants and many dangerous animals.

But it's not just high school students who show their ignorance. My cousin Bachire, who came to the United States to attend college, also gets asked ridiculous questions. His classmates wanted to know how he got here, maybe thinking that we don't have airplanes in Africa. My cousin told them that he swam the Atlantic Ocean to the U.S., and he said they believed him.

From the time I arrived in New York a few years ago, I've been surprised at how little the people here know about Africa. One day at my sister's braiding shop on Nostrand Avenue in Brooklyn, one of her clients asked us if we wear shoes in Africa.

One day, I brought pictures of Senegal to school. My classmates couldn't believe their eyes.

Of course Africans wear shoes! In Dakar, people wear Nikes, Jordans and other brand names. It irritates me that people think all of Africa is just as it was 200 years ago. Most things you can buy here in the U.S., we can buy in Senegal.

Still, when people have questions about Africa, I think it's best to answer them — or at least not make up ridiculous answers. Telling lies doesn't help educate people about the place I love. So I try to respond to questions by teaching the people who ask them a little bit about my life there.

One day, I brought pictures of my city in Senegal to school. I told my classmates that more than 2 million people live in Dakar, which has tall, modern apartment and office buildings. There are cafés and clubs that get lively once the sun goes down.

My classmates couldn't believe their eyes. They all started saying, "Is this Africa?"

"I thought it was like a jungle with elephants!" one student said. "I'll tell my father, so I can go and visit there one day."

I told her she was welcome to visit our house in Senegal any time she wanted to go. I made the offer because my family is generous, although that isn't unusual in Senegal. Senegal's nickname is "Reewu Teranga," which means "generous country" in my language, Wolof.

We like to welcome people into our homes and give them something to eat. I can visit and eat at any of my neighbors' houses anytime.

It's also a tradition for rich people to help the poor by giving them money and food. Because my family is relatively well off, we've been able to help other people. When I was about 8, a lady who neither my mom nor my dad knew used to come to our house and we gave her food, water, and clothes to wear.

American TV shows made me believe that everyone in the U.S. was rich and there weren't any homeless people.

After many years, she became like family and started calling my mom her sister-in-law. Calling someone your sister-in-law or your sister even when they aren't is not unusual in Senegal.

Sometimes such generosity can be too much. When it's time to eat, you must eat no matter what, because your host will keep insisting until you do. That has happened to me many times and I hate it, because sometimes I don't feel like eating and they won't let me be.

People eat sitting on mats on the floor with their legs crossed. They use their hands to take food from big, shared plates. We eat *thieb bou dienn* (rice and fish with vegetables) and yassa (chicken cooked with onion sauce mixed with white rice).

I like the climate in Senegal. There's a short winter from December to February, but it never snows. It only rains in summer, which is from June to November. Summers aren't that bad, even for people who don't own air conditioners. Many people in Dakar have balconies, so even if it doesn't cool down at night, people can sleep outside on their balconies.

Although it bothers me that many Americans know none of these good things about my country, I can't really blame them for thinking the way they do. What they see on TV influences what they think about Africa. If they're not watching shows about lions and antelopes on The Discovery Channel or Animal Planet, they're seeing programs about the ugly parts of the continent and the hungriest and sickest people who live there.

I know there is great poverty in Africa. Not all rich people help the poor. We need more government aid to feed people and get them jobs. But that's not all there is to say about my continent.

I understand how misleading TV can be. It influenced what I thought about the U.S. before I got here. When I was in Senegal, I watched a lot of American movies, including *Home Alone* and *American Pie*, and TV shows like *Baywatch*. Everything I saw made me believe that the U.S. was the most perfect country in the world. I thought it was a place where people partied a lot, everyone was rich, and there weren't any homeless people.

I didn't know that many people here are immigrants or the children of immigrants from all over the world. I didn't know that there are a lot of poor people and that there are ghettos. I started to learn more about the U.S. when I was 11, after two college students from Wisconsin came to live with us for six months. We gave them Senegalese names: Aicha and Biguee.

They told us that the U.S. wasn't like we imagined. They said that in the U.S., "time is money" and everyone is busy. When I came here at age 13, I saw that they were right and that life in the U.S. can be hard. The myths I'd believed about the U.S. were shattered.

After being here for four years, I've learned that the U.S. can be a hard place for everyone, especially immigrants. You can't get money when you don't work. Getting to know the country and learning the language is very difficult. Life in the U.S. can be pleasant because of the tremendous opportunities, but it's hard for many immigrants.

If I go back to Senegal after living in the U.S. for a while, I'll get to teach other people who didn't get the chance to come here. I'll teach them about the good and the bad parts of living here, because I don't want them to be disappointed if they come here.

And as long as I live here, I realize I'll always have to teach people about my country. So the next time someone asks me if we wear shoes or live with animals in Africa, I will sit them down and show them pictures of me in Africa. Hopefully, the more I teach, the fewer people will ask those kinds of questions.

Aissata was 18 when she wrote this story.

Tongue-Tied

By Amy Huang

"Awww, man," I thought to myself as my cousin Lin handed me my vocabulary list for the day: table, fish, supermarket. The words seemed never-ending, but I picked up my pencil and started copying them. That's what I did every weekend of 4th grade and the summer after.

When I was 9, my family moved to the U.S. from China. I didn't know any English, but because of my age, I was put into 4th grade. I was scared; I didn't even know the alphabet! My other cousin, who spoke English, asked the school officials to put me in a lower grade, but they refused.

I was relieved to meet three girls in my class who, though they were American born, had Chinese backgrounds: Sue, Linda, and Marie. They were the only ones I could communicate with, because they spoke Chinese. The teacher told them to show me around the school and help me adjust.

Nobody else in my class cared to talk to me or be friendly. I felt unwelcome, but I wasn't surprised. I mean, why would anyone talk to a stranger who can't speak the language? Why help someone learn?

Linda, Sue, and Marie seemed nice at first. I felt good being able to speak to kids from my own culture because it made me feel like I fit in and had friends.

A few weeks later, though, I found out that they made fun of me behind my back. I was sitting next to Sue when I saw her writing a letter to her friend, telling her how she hated me and how stupid I was. Although I couldn't read English well, I knew enough to figure out what she wrote. I felt betrayed because I thought she was my friend.

I felt betrayed and disappointed because people from my own culture had turned against me.

Then it got worse. Sue called me "sei chuen," which is like a Chinese version of "dumb-ass," right to my face. And several times, Linda deliberately spilled water on me from her water bottle.

That made me angry. I wanted to tell the teacher to get Linda in trouble, but I had no idea how to express myself. I had no choice but to try to avoid her.

What really made me upset was what they did to me during recess. Sometimes the three of them would come up to me with three other Chinese-American friends. One of them would sneak up behind me and grab my hair clip.

Then they'd run around and toss my hair clip from one person to another to keep it away from me. The torture didn't stop until the end of recess. I felt I was like playing monkey in the middle with enemies that I couldn't beat.

All I did was tell them weakly in Chinese, "Give it back." I was frustrated because I couldn't do anything else, and I felt alone because I didn't have anyone there to help me. I felt like crying, but I didn't. I refused to give them the satisfaction of knowing they'd hurt me. Plus, I felt embarrassed about letting other students see my tears.

I felt betrayed and disappointed because people from my own culture had turned against me. It felt like being smacked across the face by my own hand. I wondered why they had to pick on me. Maybe they thought it was fun to pick on a new kid, or maybe they felt superior to me because they were "Americans" and I was a foreigner.

I hated myself for not being able to speak English, since I couldn't do anything about my bullies because of that. I didn't say anything to my teacher because I thought, "What chances do I have against Sue, Linda, and Marie, who can speak English and probably would deny everything I'd say?"

I tried telling my parents about it, but it was like going to a dentist when you have a stomachache. "Just tell them to stop bothering you and stay away from them," they advised. I thought to myself, "Yeah, right, like they'll do what I say."

I was forced to put up with their bullying the rest of the year. That summer, though, I worked hard to learn English. Every day, I memorized my vocabulary and was tested on it by my cousin. As I learned more vocabulary, I asked my cousin to speak English around me instead of Chinese. A few weeks later, I was able to talk to her in English.

When I entered 5th grade, I was able to express myself and make friends, which made me feel more American. I felt like I was fitting in. I was a lot happier. And fortunately, none of my tormentors were in my class.

I also progressed in school. In 4th grade, when I was still struggling with the language, I was unable to complete my class work and homework. Since I couldn't understand my teacher, I paid no attention to what she said.

But in 5th grade, I found myself listening carefully to my teacher's words. I did my homework every night and had a strong desire to achieve. I found myself going to the library and opening myself up to a whole new world as I borrowed and read young adult novels like the *Babysitter's Club* and *Goosebumps* series.

Reading those books not only improved my reading skills, it introduced me to American culture. I learned that Americans are into sports like baseball and football. American kids roller-skate and hang out at parks, movie theaters, and pizzerias.

I found myself being slowly absorbed into American culture, watching baseball and eating hamburgers and hot dogs. I liked becoming Americanized; it helped me make friends outside of my own background. The memory of being bullied faded. But because of what I went through in 4th grade, I told myself, "I will never make fun of anyone who can't speak English." Since then, if my friends make a comment about a person who can't speak the language well, I ignore them and try to change the subject.

Because of what I went through, I told myself, "I will never make fun of anyone who can't speak English."

Ironically, however, sometimes I can't help but feel annoyed at my own family members who can't speak English. Every month when the bills arrive, I have to explain to my mom or dad what they say. I often get frustrated because I'm not very good at translating business terms like "interest" or "suspension" into Chinese, and my parents seem unable to understand what I'm saying.

"Shame on you! How can you not know how to translate after all these years you have been to school?" my parents yell when I can't give them a full translation.

"Going to school doesn't mean that I know everything," I say angrily.

A few months ago, my dad asked me to help him prepare for his naturalization exam. I didn't like doing it because I had to repeat myself many, many times before he managed to understand or memorize what I'd said.

"How do you read this question?" my dad asked.

"It says, 'Who wrote "The Star-Spangled Banner"?'" I said.

"What? Say that again. Say it slower."

"Who. . . wrote. . . the. . . Star. . . Spangled. . . Banner?" I repeated.

"Who wrote deh sta spagul banna?" my dad repeated.

"No, Dad, it's 'Star-Spangled Banner,'" I said, with gritted teeth.

"Star-Spangled Banner," he tried again.

"Yes, that's it," I said.

"What is it again?" he asked.

"THE STAR-SPANGLED BANNER!"

I was really annoyed and angry because I couldn't understand why he was so slow in understanding me. My mom noticed how impatient I was and got extremely upset. Not for the first time, she gave me a lecture on being nice and helping people.

"Don't think you're better than others just because you know some English," she scolded. "You needed help getting where you are, too."

I felt guilty even without my mother's scolding. I feel really bad when I look back on that moment, because I should've been more understanding. I am impatient and find it hard to stay calm when I'm asked to repeat the same thing over and over again, even though the way I learned English was through constant repetition. I should've thought about how much harder it was for my dad to learn English than me, because he's a lot older and he doesn't go to school.

I'm hoping that, next time, when I'm asked to make explanations to others who can't understand English, I'll be more patient and less irritated. It's hard to control emotions, but I'll try. I was helpless once myself and I know how awful it felt.

Amy was 15 when she wrote this story.

Becoming A Different Person

By Daniel Verzhbo

I remember looking out the plane's window and seeing how beautiful America looked. I couldn't wait to be in New York City among all those tall buildings. I expected America to be a very good country. I pictured my mom and me having a good life, ready to overcome anything.

But when we got to America, it wasn't as perfect as it looked. In Russia I was a good, quiet kid, always staying at home and spending time with my family. But in America, I started to become a different Daniel.

When we got to New York my mom got a job as a cleaning lady, but a few months later she got hurt and couldn't work anymore. Since we had no money to pay the rent, we had to go into a shelter for homeless people.

When we moved into the shelter I was very sad and depressed.

I started to miss my family. I felt sorry for myself, and even more for my mother. Our neighborhood in Brooklyn smelled like straight garbage and old buildings. Every other night I heard these loud noises that always woke me up. I thought it was fireworks at first. I also heard a lot of ambulances. "There must be lots of accidents around here," I thought. Later I realized that the fireworks were gunshots and the accidents were bullet wounds.

The first couple of weeks I tried to stay away from meeting new people. I felt unsure of myself in this new life, and I didn't have the confidence to go out and look for friends. I was shy and used to keeping to myself. In Russia, I never needed to meet new people because I had my family. There were six of us and we were like a team, always together and always looking out for each other. I felt safe, and knew that with my family behind me I could accomplish anything I set my mind to.

But now I was in America, and I didn't have all that to back me up. I didn't even know the language very well. Now that I only had my mother I was lonely and bored. I got tired of sitting in the small room that my mother and I had to share. I also got tired of trying to tell myself that I had something, because I really had nothing. No family, no friends—no life.

My friends opened the door for me to the real world, outside of my room. I felt like I was finally fitting in in America.

One day as I was shooting baskets by myself a couple of kids came over. "Yo, you look like you play ball, you want to run a full court with us?" one of them asked.

I was scared, and I barely understood him because my English was so poor. But I knew the words "full court." In my school kids would always say those words when they were playing ball. I thought this could be a new way to meet friends. But I played horribly and barely even scored. I was angry at myself.

"I let the opportunity slide right by me," I thought. "I played so badly nobody will even talk to me."

But after the game one kid introduced himself, and I met all of them one by one. I was relieved to see that they weren't going to rob me.

I started playing basketball and hanging out with those guys on a regular basis, and I started to feel more comfortable around them. Finally, I had friends. They opened the door for me to the real world, outside of my room. I started to feel good about myself. I felt like I was finally fitting in in America.

I started to do the things my friends did, like smoke cigarettes, and steal small things like candy from the store. I thought, "It's just candy. What's the worst that could happen?"

After a few months my mother and I moved to a nicer shelter in Sheepshead Bay, Brooklyn, and I made a new friend. Darren lived in my building, and hanging out with him made me feel comfortable about myself. I could relate to him because we'd both been through a lot of the same things. We both had single mothers and didn't have a lot of money.

Darren introduced me to his crew. They were mad cool, and at first it felt good to be around them. Hanging out with them was like being part of a huge family. I felt protected. But the crew also got me involved in some bad stuff like smoking weed, fighting, and stealing.

The first time I smoked weed I thought that it would make me cough, like cigarettes, but it felt smooth as I inhaled it. I felt that "chillin feelin" (as my friends used to call it) that the weed gives you after the first couple of pulls. That feeling took me to another world. I loved it.

After that I started to smoke daily and do stupid stuff with the crew. We'd pick on other kids and run from the police. Sometimes it felt good to be reckless with them. I liked the excitement. And hurting others seemed to get my own pain off my shoulders. It still hurt to be away from my family, and I felt alone, even when I was with my crew. No friends of mine could give me the love that I'd left behind in Russia.

When I chilled with the crew we looked like a gang and lots of people were scared of us. Sometimes I didn't like that, because I didn't feel like myself. But it made me feel safe on the streets. After a while, I didn't feel scared of anything.

My mom could see the crew was a bad influence and tried her best to prevent me from hanging out with them. She would lock me inside the house, or find other things for me to do after school like swimming or a soccer team. At first, I listened and did everything that she asked me to do. But as time went on I started to get bored, and I didn't feel like following my mom's rules anymore. It was fun being stupid and not caring about anything. For the first time of my life, I was a bad ass.

Besides, being high all the time stopped me from thinking too much. I stopped worrying about my mom, and every time I smoked weed I would remember my family in Russia less and less.

One day my mom caught me smoking a cigarette and humiliated me right in front of my friends. First she slapped the cigarette out my hands and then she started to yell at me. I didn't know whether to be mad at myself for not listening to my mom or at her for humiliating me in front of my friends like that. I decided to be mad at her.

Every time I smoked weed I would remember my family in Russia less and less.

I started coming home very late, and sometimes not coming home at all. My mother kept on giving me punishments, but they weren't affecting my behavior. I wasn't a little kid who was scared to get hit with a belt anymore. I started to steal money from my mother to get more weed.

I loved my mom with all my heart, and stealing from her felt like stealing from myself. It hurt. But when I bought and smoked weed with the money that I stole, the pain went away. That cycle continued. My relationship with my mother started to fade, while my relationship with my friends got stronger.

Soon I was getting into lots of fights and stealing stuff on a regular basis. That weed that I was smoking was making my life miserable, but most of the time I was too high to notice. For me, smoking wasn't the problem. The real problem was getting money.

One of my friends and I started stealing collector cards from Toys "R" Us and selling them on the Internet. I'd never stolen that much before, and for the first time something inside of me told me that stealing wasn't the right thing to do. I wasn't used to that feeling. But since I really needed the money, I didn't let it bother me.

I started to steal more and more. Then one day I stole about $95 worth of cards and got caught. I started to cry because I thought it was the end of the world. I'd never in my life been handcuffed in a police car. I was terrified at the thought of going to jail.

When my mom picked me up from the precinct she looked so depressed. I didn't know what to say. I thought she was going to yell at me and give me lots of punishments. But she wasn't saying anything to me at all. She was just looking out the window and I could see on her face that she was thinking very hard about something.

After we got home I told her that I was really sorry, and that my punishment should be very big. But she told me there wasn't going to be a punishment.

"I'm not going to punish you because you are old enough to control yourself and to think about your life," she said. "You are 14 years old, getting locked up and smoking weed."

For some reason I couldn't get those words out of my head: "You are old enough." What did that mean? Was I becoming older and maturing? Was I supposed to know how to survive by myself?

"It's like I'm becoming this monster," I thought to myself. "My mom looks so stressed. It looks like she's going through more pain than me." I felt like everything started to change against me. My shoulders felt very heavy, and my conscience started to burn me alive.

I wish I could say that was the day I started to straighten my life out. But it was just the beginning of the bad side of my life. It would take me about two years to come back to this world and find the real me that I'd been looking for for years. I would never be that same perfect kid from Russia, but I found out how to be someone who feels good about himself and the life he's living in.

That night, I was really thinking about the person I had become, and how I wanted to change. But the next day I was too depressed to think about anything. So I dealt with it the way I always did — I got some weed, and got my mind out of this world.

Daniel was 16 when he wrote this story.

Jose Mercado

Rich Country, Hard Life

By Raquel Fernandes

When my mother came to America, I was only 10 years old. She left my brothers and me behind in Brazil with my grandmother, and I was very angry because I felt she didn't care about us anymore.

She returned two years later asking my father's permission to bring one of my brothers and me to the United States. I wanted to go because I missed her very much. But it took her two more years to convince my father to let us go, and also to save money for a place with enough room for all of us.

Although I had missed my mother a lot in the beginning, when my father told me I would finally be joining her in the United States, I felt confused. My first response was, "I'm not going," because I had grown used to my mother's absence. I was 15 by then and had established a life of my own in Brazil. I had a large bedroom with my own TV and a piano. I hung out every day with my friends, and because of the warm weather, we could play in the streets until nighttime all year round. We lived in a safe, clean neighborhood in the city of Rio de Janeiro.

My father convinced me it would be better to be with my mother than away from her. I knew I was giving up a lot. But since I had a very good life in Brazil and I knew the United States is a much richer country, I figured life in the U.S. would be even better.

I wasn't prepared for how completely my life changed when I moved here. I didn't know anyone and I couldn't speak English, so I was afraid to go anywhere after school by myself. Since my mother had to work all day, I just went to school and came straight home.

Our home itself was another shock. Instead of being an improvement over our home in Brazil, our apartment here was much smaller. I didn't even have my own bedroom anymore—I had to share with my brother.

I had imagined that everything here in New York would be clean and sparkling, but it wasn't as nice as where I had lived in Rio. In Brazil, my building had a swimming pool and a nice outside play area for kids. Here there's nowhere to hang out except the streets or someone's house.

Although I haven't always been happy here, I have matured a lot from the independence I've had to develop.

I felt afraid and uncomfortable because I noticed people staring at me in the train station and on the streets, and at school kids would make fun of me and ask me questions like, "Why do you dress this way?" because I wore tight pants and shirts. Now I wear clothes one or two sizes bigger than my size so I won't attract attention. Kids also called me names and said I was not black because I spoke and looked different from them (I am light skinned).

Things like this never happened to me in Brazil. There,

everybody was kind and helped me with everything. The teachers would worry if you weren't doing your homework. Here, it seems they just take care of their business and you have to watch out for yourself.

In Brazil, my parents let me go out whenever I wanted because we knew our neighbors and always had people looking out for us. Neighbors helped each other all the time. We don't have that feeling of security here. Our neighbors come from so many different countries they have nothing in common.

I have neighbors from Colombia, Egypt, Greece, and Korea. Many of them probably couldn't communicate with one another if they wanted to. Besides, they work so many hours every day they probably don't even know who lives across the street. They have to spend a lot of time working to accomplish what they came here for.

Although I came here expecting our life to be as good or better than what we left behind, I know now that it is not easy to build a new life. But I have learned some valuable lessons by coming here. My mother, brother and I have learned to survive on our own in ways we never had to in Brazil, where things were very easy for us.

Looking back, I see how materialistic I was when I lived in Brazil. I have learned from this experience that one day you can have everything and the next day it can all be gone. I also understand why my mother had to come by herself and work long days and nights to lay the foundation for us.

Although I haven't always been happy here, I have matured a lot from the independence I've had to develop. If I were still in Brazil I probably would not be able to do things on my own, like travel alone on subways to school and elsewhere. In your own country, you see the same people and do the same things every day. You stay in your own little world and your experience doesn't grow.

This summer I'm going to go back and visit Brazil for the first time since I left. I know that it will not seem the same to me, and the people I know there will also see me differently now. They'll see that I've changed.

I don't even know if I'm going to have the same friends because after all the things that have happened to me here, I don't know if my old friends and I will think the same way anymore.

And I know I'll miss New York: the way we live here, the rush, the trains, the responsibilities I have everyday. I think I'm going to start feeling bored. It may seem surprising after all I've said, but when I go back, I don't think I will want to stay.

Raquel was 17 when she wrote this story.

Chapter 2:
What We Left Behind

Cezary Ladocha

Moonlit Memories

By Chun Lar Tom

One evening, back in China, my little sister Bik Bik and I sat in front of our house to wait for the moon. An hour later, it rose in the sky. The village became beautiful and charming in the softness of the moonlight.

That evening, Bik Bik and I helped Mom set up a table in the open air near our house and the rest of the people in our village set up tables, too. We ate dishes like chicken and river snails with red pepper. After dinner, Father set off firecrackers and burned incense to welcome the goddess of the moon, or The Moon Lady.

This was how we celebrated the Moon Festival in China, also called Mid-Autumn Day (Zhong Qiu Jie). It's usually held at night during a full moon on the fifteenth day of the eighth lunar month. That night, the moon is believed to be at its brightest and roundest for the year. The Chinese consider this the best time to

45

celebrate the end of the harvest season with a big feast.

Mooncakes are the most important food served at Moon Festival because they symbolize the holiday. Like their name implies, mooncakes are usually round like the moon. They're served as dessert at the celebration.

To me, mooncakes also symbolized family unity and perfection. Every year at the Moon Festival, my aunts, uncles, and cousins who worked and lived miles away in the city Kaiping would come to my village of Maoping with delicious mooncakes.

I could never forget the whole family sitting at the table, eating mooncakes, chatting and laughing in the soft moonlight. It was a feeling of reunion, harmonious and joyful.

Aunt Mei laughed loudest at the table. She was a kind and happy person with a big smile on her face all the time. Cute, fat Uncle Qiang was my favorite little uncle. His big eyes shone in his round face as he told us about the circus he'd seen in the city. Then there was my cousin Yi, a sweet and quiet girl who followed me everywhere during the festival. When she smiled, two dimples lit up her ruddy oval face.

Our grandparents had told us that the Moon Lady was supposed to come down to Earth and eat the mooncakes that people prepared for her.

"Mom, how do you know the Moon Lady came down and ate the mooncakes already?" Bik Bik asked as we ate dessert. "We still have the same number of mooncakes."

"I just know it," Mom replied. Mom told us stories about the Moon Lady as well and taught us folk songs to invite her. And Grandma showed us how to make wishes to the Moon Lady. Bik Bik and I were always running around during the festival, humming songs, eating our mooncakes.

*M*y memories of the Moon Festival are some of the warmest memories I have of my family. But things changed after I came to America when I was 15. My family members and I are no longer able to get together. My aged grandparents, Aunt Mei, and Uncle Qiang are all back in China.

When the night of the Moon Festival came during my first year in America, I missed them so much, especially my grandparents. My family here can't celebrate the Moon Festival the way we used to. We can't set up a table in the open air like we did in Maoping, watching the moon as we enjoy mooncakes. And now, for dinner on the day of the festival, Mom cooks shrimp instead of river snails, because that's what's available.

We still eat mooncakes on the night of the festival. But for me, after losing my traditions,

To me, mooncakes symbolized family unity and perfection.

mooncakes can't symbolize family unity anymore. Now when I look at the designs on the cake's skin—which looked so beautiful back in Maoping—they seem like little cracks that'll split the cake apart. The mooncakes' roundness reminds me that my family is no longer round and whole.

During the last mooncake celebration I had with my family, I looked up into the dark blue sky, mooncake in hand. The moon looked less bright and less round than it had in China. Taking a small bite of the mooncake, I heard my grandmother's soft voice coming from overseas: "Chun Lar, make your wish to the Moon Lady. It will come true."

I stared at the moon and made my wish: "I wish my family will be reunited for the next Moon Festival."

Chun Lar was 18 when she wrote this story.
She went on to attend Bard College.

Stephen Adler

No Place to Call Home

By Mohammad Ali

All my life, my family has been searching for a home. We lived in Baghdad, Iraq, during the Persian Gulf War in 1991, with bombs falling around us. Then we had to sneak out of the country into Jordan, where my father was not allowed to work. Finally, we tried to find a home in Europe—but ended up almost being sent to our death.

My name is Mohammad Ali and I am not a boxer. I come from the Middle East and I am Kurdish.

The Kurds are an ethnic group that doesn't have a country to call its own. There are more than 25 million Kurds, and we mostly live in the mountainous parts of Turkey, Iran, and Iraq. This area used to be called Kurdistan, but before World War I, we lost our land.

Ever since then we've been fighting to get it back. We have our own culture, and we want to be able to live according to our customs. But the countries Kurds have lived in are racist, and they have not granted us equal rights. In Iraq, it was illegal to have a Kurdish school, or to teach your kids how to write and read Kurdish. Many Kurds were killed because they wouldn't renounce who they are.

When I was young, I went to the region we still call Kurdistan three times. You cannot imagine how beautiful the place was. The house my family rented had a small orchard with different fruit trees, and a small stream ran around the house. I felt that I belonged to this place. But instead of living there, my family was always looking for a home. Sometimes I feel ashamed when people ask me, "Where are you from?" I just say to them that I do not have a country.

I was born in Kuwait and so were my parents, but there people speak Arabic and not my language, Kurdish. Once I asked my father, "Why we are in this country and not in our native country?" My father told me how my grandfather had moved from Kurdistan to Kuwait more than 40 years earlier because Kurdistan is very poor. In Kuwait, my family had a good life.

Sometimes I feel ashamed when people ask, "Where are you from?" I just say I do not have a country.

But in 1989 we moved to Iraq, where my father had some relatives. Iraq is north of Kuwait and south of Turkey. Like Kuwait, it is a country rich with oil. Baghdad was beautiful then. My house was big, and outside we had a garden scented with the sweet fragrance of jasmine flowers. My parents' faces were so happy that, if you saw them, you would know they were thinking, "Wow, this will be our country." They dreamed we could make Iraq our home.

Our lives were good until Iraq started a war with Kuwait

because Saddam Hussein, Iraq's leader, wanted their oil fields. To get their homeland back, Kuwait called for help from the U.S., and the Gulf War began in 1990. It didn't last long, but in Iraq, people suffered a lot from the bombs and from not having food, electricity, or medicine for a long time after the bombing stopped.

At the time of the war I was about 7 years old. The U.S. was bombing Iraq in the morning and in the night. The first attack was on the electricity building, and the power went out for the rest of the year. My house used to shake every time a bomb hit the ground, and when the house shook more, that meant that the bomb was closer to where I lived.

Everything was scary. I used to stay home all the time, sometimes inside the garage or the garden. It felt like jail. I used to sleep when the sun set and wake up at sunrise because we had no lights.

In those days, life felt like a dark sky. During the war most countries stopped trading with Iraq, so there was very little food or medicine in the country. People couldn't work, so they sold their cars and things from their houses. Still, they were starving.

After the war Iraq was powerless, and the Kurds started to take back much of their land in the north. Their land is the most beautiful part of Iraq—green and mountainous. Saddam Hussein knew that if the Kurds were to get back all of their land for good, he would lose much of Iraq. He began killing Kurds, whether they lived in the north or in Baghdad; eventually his government killed more than 15,000 Kurds.

I had felt that Iraq was my country, but my feelings changed when the people and the Iraqi government showed their feelings toward Kurds after the war. I felt that I was not Iraqi, but a Kurd.

My family escaped the killings, but Saddam Hussein also made a law to make all the Kurds leave Baghdad and go to the south and west of Iraq—to the desert. Those places were dangerous and very poor, so my father said we had to leave Iraq. At the time, the only place Iraqis could go was Jordan. It cost a lot to go, and we had to sneak out of Iraq to get there.

It was a long way to Jordan, more than a day's journey by bus along a highway surrounded by black rock. But once we got there, the first few months were like heaven. I had almost everything I wanted. I was always with my two cousins and my brother, going around the city.

To me this life was cool, but my parents did not feel the same way. They wanted to get out of Jordan because we were being discriminated against. My father wasn't allowed to work and I wasn't allowed to go to school, because we were considered only temporary refugees; after six months, Iraqi passport holders had to pay a little each day they remained in Jordan. Besides this, the police were racist and would mistreat those who weren't Jordanian citizens. Sometimes they would send them back to their home countries.

I was afraid Jordan would be the final chapter of my life's book, and the end would be in Iraq.

My father wanted to go to Europe, where he had friends who seemed to have good lives. So he got us fake visas and we didn't tell anyone that we were leaving until the last minute. We got on the plane without problems, and I felt like I was on top of the world. I was wishing for a new life where everything would be perfect.

But when we landed in Hungary and went through customs, the officials found out the visas were fake. My legs were heavy; I couldn't stand. I hoped it was just a dream and that they would wake me up before it became real.

They put us in a refugee camp and kept us there for 21 days. It was like a jail: eating your lunch, then going back to your room or watching the TV. After three weeks, the Hungarian authorities made us leave the country. We flew to Egypt, then to Greece, looking for a place where we would be allowed to stay. Finally we were sent back to Jordan. We had heard that people like us who were sent back there had been killed. I was so scared getting off the plane in Jordan; I was afraid this would be the final chapter of my life's book, and the end would be in Iraq.

My father asked the Jordanian airport officials to call the United Nations to help us. At first, they told us a car was coming to take us to Iraq, and we were all thinking how we would kill ourselves before we'd let that happen. But a while later, a man came from the UN to talk to us. We told him everything we'd been through, and when he made calls to investigate our story, he found that it was true.

We were told the UN would grant us refugee status, but first we had to wait. So we stayed for about three weeks in the Jordan airport. The men slept in a waiting room, and my mother, sister, and youngest brother slept in a small room in a women's bathroom. After that, the UN began giving us money so we could stay in Jordan temporarily, and I was allowed to go to school. I was happy because I'd been out of school for almost two years.

A few weeks after I finished the year, my family was granted entry to the United States. We were so excited. Everybody in Jordan said to us, "You will have the best life."

People in the Middle East were always talking about America. They said that when you come here, the government gives you a house and money every month. They said you don't have to work, only go to school and have a lot of time with your relatives. I believed them. I was excited to move here and make America my home.

When we first got here, though, my aunt—who had been living here for six or seven years—told us how hard our lives would be. For the first few days we stayed with her. She had a nice apartment, a car, and enough money to send to her family back home, but like most immigrants, she had to earn everything she had.

During those first few days, I went to Manhattan and admired the reflection of the sun on all the tall glass towers. Seeing all the beautiful houses and new cars in my aunt's neighborhood made me feel that it would only be a matter of time until I could have a good life like everyone else in America.

But when we moved into the apartment my aunt found for us, we were shocked. It was small, old, and full of mice and cockroaches. We slept without blankets and pillows, and furnished the house with things from the garbage: an old TV, a carpet, and some other furniture.

It was a big shock for my family to be living in worse conditions than we knew in Jordan. My mom began saying she wanted to go back. My dad was quiet.

Our relatives didn't believe that we didn't have money. They think that if you are in America, you are rich.

My aunt used to come every day and tell us this was only the beginning, and things would get better. Still, we felt lost. At least in Jordan we knew how to speak Arabic and used to get money from the UN. Here, we had no money. Yet we had relatives in Jordan who used to call us, expecting my parents to send money every week. My parents sent something when we had it, but most of the time we were too poor. Our relatives didn't believe that we didn't have money. They think that if you are in America, you are rich.

My father found work driving for a car service in Red Hook, Brooklyn. He used to come back at midnight so tired that he would only eat and then sleep until he had to go to work again. Sometimes I didn't see him all day. My mother didn't work because my younger brother was only 3, and also because in the Middle East, wives don't usually work. It was hard to get by, but we didn't want to give up our culture.

When school started, I was in 8th grade. My first week, I was scared. I thought, "How am I going to make them understand me?" I was like a statue in class. I knew only "yes," "no," and "English." When students or teachers asked me questions, I'd say, "No English."

Out of my whole class, only my sister and one other student, from Syria, could speak Arabic. I had no choice but to practice my English, and within a year, it had become my third language. I didn't speak it perfectly, but America became a better place once I could speak English. I made friends, and felt less like an outsider. I also learned about other people. I never knew that Christianity had divisions like Catholic and Protestant. And Latino people— I'd never heard of them. I was really surprised to find so many Americans speak Spanish.

But I didn't feel completely accepted. I found out that there are stereotypes about Muslims. Some people think that all Muslims are dangerous terrorists; we're not. Some of my friends used to ask me questions like, "Did you kill Jewish people? Did you bomb somebody?" I had to say, "No, no." Sometimes it made me mad, but I think people like to learn about other peoples and countries, so I'd just answer their questions honestly.

I also found there were things in American culture I didn't want to pick up, like the way kids in this country don't listen to their parents. It seems kids here have more power than adults, because parents and teachers aren't supposed to hit their kids. In the Middle East, parents hit their kids and if you have an attitude at school, teachers will hit you. I think that's why kids there are mostly good in school: They stop misbehaving after getting hit a lot. Here, when you do something wrong in school, they take you to the detention room and later you go back to class like you didn't do anything. I had friends who misbehaved just to get out of class.

Another thing that bothers me is that when a kid in the U.S. gets to 18, their parents don't always have a say in their lives anymore, and the kids usually leave their parents. In the Middle

East, most kids live at home until they get married, and then they live either with the husband or wife's parents.

I don't want to give up those aspects of my culture. But immigrant kids who came here when they were young seem much more eager to become American. Often, they don't know how to speak their parents' language, and they don't hold onto their home cultures. They say, "I'm American; that's it."

I feel glad to speak my own language at home, and read Arabic newspapers, watch Arabic TV and listen to Kurdish music. But I hate that I no longer get lessons in the Muslim religion at school. I used to take a religion class every day growing up. Now, I feel that I'm losing what I learned about the Qur'an and about the history of my people, even though I study it at home.

And I don't pray five times each day like I used to. Every Muslim is supposed to pray five times a day from the age of 7 until the last day of his or her life. In the Middle East, we used to go to a prayer room at school. Here, I know I can't leave the classroom for 15 minutes each morning and afternoon.

My parents warn me to follow my own culture while taking advantage of the good things America offers, like a good education. They talk to me about wrong and right, but what they

I feel that I'm losing what I learned about the Qur'an and the history of my people.

really want is for their kids to have a better life than the life they had. In Iraq my father was an architect, but his jobs here have been awful. He always says, "Do you want to work in a car service and be afraid all the time that you'll be killed, or do you want to be a doctor and help people?"

Still, my father wants to stay in America for the rest of his life because he is sure that this country is stable. Every year, the countries in the Middle East seem to get worse. I think the situation won't improve in those countries until we stop having dictators there, and begin using the same system as the United States—with institutions like the Supreme Court, Congress, and an elected president—so no one will have too much power.

I intend to go to college in America, but every day I think of moving back to the Middle East and staying for the rest of my life. I really want to live in the north of Iraq where there are Kurds. I hope in the future that I will have a country, but I know that Kurdistan won't be a country unless the United States were to force the Middle East to give land back to the Kurds. I don't think that will happen. So I think I will never have a land I can truly call my own.

Mohammad was 16 when he wrote this story.

Elizabeth Deegan

Saying Goodbye

By Agelta Arqimandriti

I grew up in Tirana, the capital of Albania. It's small, but it looks a little like New York, filled with yelling people, vendors selling things everywhere in the street, and honking cars.

My country, though, was very dangerous when I lived there. In the streets I saw many terrible things. I saw people wearing black masks and carrying machine guns. They would point their weapons at the sky and shoot them to scare everyone.

The people in my country were angry with one another and willing to kill for nothing. Everyone there was poor, too, and when people don't have food, they will sell everything they own to get some.

My family and I were lucky—my parents both had jobs, and eventually we were able to move to New York for a better life. I thought once we moved here, life would be easy. But for my family and me, it has been difficult and disappointing. Life in New York is hard because we have to work so much, and we feel kind of lonely because we don't speak English well.

When I tell people that the life here is difficult, they ask me, "What did you know about America before you came here?" And I don't like to give an answer, but I had been thinking that life would be simple here, because America is a powerful country.

The hardest thing has been losing the friends I had in Albania. Even though life there could be awful, I felt comforted by the people I knew. Now, whenever my friends write me letters, they make me cry because they write about the happy times in our past when we went on trips and had fun. And they write that they miss me so much.

My best friend was Jonila, who I met when I was in the 1st grade. One day we had difficult homework and she asked me if we could do the homework together. After that, she gave me her phone number and we started talking every day. She liked the same things I did, like watching TV, listening to music, reading, and going outside to play.

No one talked to me because I did not speak English. All day at school I was alone, as if no one else was in the room.

On her block we had lots of other friends, and I would always go to her block and talk and play with everyone there. She always wanted to have fun and smile, and she didn't ever stay sad. In hard times, she was always telling funny stories. She made other people smile.

Our houses were far apart, so we called each other often. For a while, we both watched a serial movie (like a soap opera) on TV, and each day when it was over, we would call each other and talk about what had happened in the movie. It was a beautiful and romantic story, and we loved to talk about it.

When I left my country, I was in the 8th grade. On my last day of school, my friends and I started to cry. To make fun, one friend told me, "We've had almost our whole lives together, and it's better to go now because I want other friends in my life and not only you." She wanted to make my friends smile. I smiled too, but I felt very sad saying goodbye.

Before I left for the United States, my friends and I had a beautiful Christmas party, where we ate pizza and lollipops and traditional Albanian foods. We danced to the guitar and piano music of my country.

Now, when I listen to this music, I think of our party and feel a little bit sad. Sometimes I lie in my bed, thinking about my past, and I wonder when I can go to my country for a visit. Any time I think about my best friend, I feel far away from everyone, and so alone. We still keep in touch, but we are not as close anymore.

*I*n this country I feel like a stranger, because I don't have any close friends. When I started school here, no one talked to me because I did not speak English. All day at school I was alone, as if no one else was in the room. I felt uncomfortable and sad.

My school has immigrants from many different countries, but I think these people quickly forget what it was like when they first came here, since they didn't try to talk to me or make me feel at home. Instead, they sometimes laughed at me.

My second day of school here, somebody liked my sneakers and she asked me, "What is your size?" I misunderstood what she said and I told her, "I buy that for $60." Everyone who heard me laughed. That day made me hate school, and I didn't want to go anymore.

When I got home, I said to my parents, "I don't want to live here. I am the unluckiest girl in the whole world."

My parents told me, "Don't worry, this will pass. Eventually you will learn English and everything will be fine." Their words made me feel a little bit happier and more relaxed.

They were right, because now that I have worked hard to learn English, I am doing better. Now when I go to school I feel happier because I have made some friends. When I can't understand something, I ask somebody, and they try to help me. I also met a girl from my country, and we understand each other very well.

But so far, I don't have a best friend who I can talk to about the personal things in my life. Maybe when my English is perfect, I will find someone to be close with. But for now, I don't have the connection to anyone here that I used to have with my friends at home.

And in this country, my family life has changed. In my country, my parents had easy work. My father worked in the post office and he enjoyed it. Here, he works long hours in a department store and has to stand up all day. My mom works in a factory here and she is tired, too. They never have free time anymore.

I think my future here will be easier than in Albania, because in my country, many people don't have jobs. They have to struggle for everything. Few people can afford to go to college. Young people who don't go to college have to search for work, which they can't always find, so they end up staying home. Many families don't have enough to eat.

I'm glad to have left the dangers of my country, but we also left the comforts of home.

Life here is easier in so many ways. If I get good grades, I can go to college, even if I don't have too much money. Here I have many opportunities, and I feel sure that when I finish college, I can find a good job and have a bright future.

Still, it has been very hard for me and my family to adjust to the big changes in our lives. We didn't expect it. I'm glad to have left the dangers of my country, but we also left the comforts of home. I need to work very hard to be as happy and relaxed as I was in my own country.

I hope that when I finish college, I can go and work in my

country for a few years. I would love to leave right now and continue high school there with my old friends, but I can't. Life in my country is too difficult and dangerous. I'm hoping that one day the situation in my country will be good and my family and I can go back.

Agelta was 17 when she wrote this story.

Kaite Martin

A Goat Named Manush

By David Etienne

People from the city in Haiti sometimes make fun of Haitian country people and their accents. But I think country people are smarter than city people. For one thing, city people depend on food grown and transported by others, but country people are self-sufficient and grow their own.

This isn't always easy, as I learned a few years ago. I lived in a rural town called Diegue. When I turned 7, my godmother gave me a baby goat. I had never dreamed of getting a goat for my birthday, and I was so happy. The goat was brown with a little bit of white on her face.

At first I left the goat untied, because I wanted her to follow me around, until one day a man who lived nearby came to my house with a machete. He explained that the goat had eaten his crops, and if he found her in his garden ever again he would cut off her head. I decided it would be a good idea to tie my goat.

This goat and I became great friends. I even ate my dinner near her and fed her some of my rice. My older cousin, Fabian, also loved taking care of the goat and gave her the name "Manush." I liked it, so the goat now had a name. I promised my cousin that one day I would give her a baby goat like my godmother gave me.

After some time, we took Manush to a place where they had male goats and paid the owner to leave her there for one day. After a few months, she had three babies. I really wanted to give my cousin one, but I couldn't bear to give up any of them, so I asked her to wait until Manush had other babies.

After two years I had about seven goats and all of them were friendly. But I had a special relationship with Manush. Some people say that dogs are man's best friend, but this female goat was mine.

On my 10th birthday, my mother asked me if I wanted to eat one of the goats for my birthday. At that time nothing was in my mind except that I was about to eat a lot of meat, which I loved so much. Goat meat is one of the most expensive meats in Haiti and I felt honored to have a whole goat cooked just for my birthday.

I held the legs, but before my godfather could even put the knife on the goat, I started crying.

When my godfather was about to kill the goat (not Manush), he called me so I could hold its feet while he cut it under the throat. I was excited—some other kids were watching and this made me feel more grown-up and important than them.

I held the goat's legs, but before my godfather could even put the knife on the goat, I started crying. My hands were shaking. I suddenly felt as if the life of one of my best friends was about to be taken away. I felt weak and guilty knowing that I was going to play a part in killing my goat.

My older brother called me soft, and made me go away

for the rest of the day. I went into the woods where I had put Manush and the rest of the goats. As soon as Manush saw me she started trying to come near me. I walked to her and petted her for a while.

I was thinking about the goat's head being cut off its body. To me it felt like a crime. Eventually my sister came to get me. I went home and sat at the table alone. Everyone was watching me as I ate the food, including the meat, with anger and sadness.

I tried hard not to let the goat's death affect me because I knew if I didn't get over it, my family and friends would make fun of me. On my next birthday they wanted to kill Manush but I wouldn't let them, so they killed another of Manush's babies. Even though the goats belonged to me, I had no choice about this because everyone was looking forward to the goat meat and the great-tasting soup my mother would make from it.

I left Haiti for New York City one spring day when I was 12. Two nights before I left, I went into the yard where the goats were and sat there talking to Manush. I knew I wasn't going to have any time to say goodbye if I didn't do it then. I felt like crying, but I didn't. I sat there petting Manush on the head, telling her that Fabian was going to take good care of her.

Now I live in a big city where it's nice not to have to eat one of my lovely goats on my birthday every March 19th. But the day still reminds me of them. It sounds thoughtful that my family would kill a goat just to please me, but my birthday has become one of the worst days of the year because I can't help thinking about the times when I had to eat creatures I cared about.

Here in New York I can find almost everything I need, except for the atmosphere of the countryside—the aroma of coffee and fresh-made bread, roosters singing in the morning, the woods. I miss my favorite friend, Manush, most of all.

Two years ago I went to Haiti for a few days. When I asked about Manush, my mother told me my godmother was watching over her, but when I asked to go see her, they never took me. That made me suspicious. Now my cousin tells me on the phone that Manush is still alive, but I don't believe her. It makes more sense that my family would sell her, because goats are worth a lot of money in Haiti.

Soon I will be going back there for another visit and I will have the chance to see for myself, but I have a bad feeling. Everyone else thought of her as just a goat, but Manush was family to me.

David was 17 when he wrote this story.
He enrolled in college after high school.

Martell Brown

Other Ways to Be Rich

By Leneli Liggayu

I felt excited but weird as I sat down to e-mail my cousin Michelle in the Philippines last June. A pang of guilt struck me as I typed. I'd had so many chances to keep in touch and yet I'd let six years go by.

"Will she write back?" I wondered. "Will she like the gifts I sent?" I finished the last line, took a deep breath, and with a shaky hand pressed "send."

I hadn't seen Michelle or my other relatives since I visited the Philippines when I was 10. I remember the moment my parents, brother and I first stepped out of the revolving airport doors into the muggy city air of Manila, the capital of the Philippines. It was crowded, the heat didn't feel clean and the humidity made my throat tighten. But the number one reason for my nervousness was meeting my family. I didn't know my relatives, and I worried they might not accept their comparatively rich American relative.

My parents, who had immigrated to the U.S. before I was born, were constantly sending medicine and clothes to my aunts and uncles in the Philippines. I always assumed they were poor and didn't have any major income besides what my parents sent.

We left the airport and took an old van to Fort Bonifacio, an hour outside Manila. Looking out the window as we drove through a few small towns, it was almost as I'd imagined it, except there were so many cars it was almost impossible to see the road below us. I also saw motorbikes pulling carriages, just a step above a horse and buggy. And the roofs of the one-room houses we passed were just wide steel panels.

I had to giggle at the image of the little pig slipping from their hands like butter.

When we got to the house, I sighed with relief because it was bigger than the ones we'd passed. The first floor was built deep into the ground, with a sewer system around it like a moat. The second floor towered up high past a mango tree. At least 15 relatives came out to greet us. They were friendly and that calmed my nerves.

But when I finally fell asleep that night, I was awakened by a lizard crawling into my bed and up to my arm. It was green and scaly and about the size of my forearm. Its eyes stared at me with interest.

My scream woke the rest of my family, and I could hear giggling in the other room. I was embarrassed because I didn't want to seem weak, but I couldn't understand how someone could sleep at night with creatures roaming all over their bed.

Soon I relaxed a little, and began to get to know my cousins for the first time. I had five girl cousins and two boy cousins ranging from age 2 to 17-year-old Michelle. They were all affectionate and accepting.

They told me stories of their daily lives that could fill books.

My 11-year-old cousins Mari and Alea told me about the time they were behind the house taking care of the baby pigs, and one slipped from their grip. He ran for the streets, fairly quickly for something with little pig legs. They chased him, but he kept getting away.

I had to giggle at the image of the little pig slipping from their hands like butter. As more and more stories flowed from their mouths, I realized they had a pretty happy life without a lot of material things. I never heard them complain about how little they had. Instead of feeling bad for them like I once had, I felt envious of all their stories and fun. Little did I know, I would soon be part of a story that I'd get to tell.

One evening, I was sitting on the couch, playing Scrabble with my uncle and two other cousins, when a voice disturbed my train of thought.

"Let me go get ready," said my grandfather Tatay (which means father in Tagalog, the main language of the Philippines). As he walked away quietly, the only sounds I heard were my aunts picking up toys off the floor as if someone important were coming.

Part of me wanted to jump in and let the floodwater take me anywhere it wanted to go.

I wasn't sure why everyone began to groan and moan. All I knew was that the floor was abnormally clean and everyone was sitting on a chair or the couch as if waiting for something. Then the sound of thunder breaking the night sky startled me. Rain pounded on the steel roof and began seeping under the door into the house.

"Come on! Let's go help Tatay!" my cousin Mari exclaimed. I didn't know what she was talking about but I ran off with her to my grandfather's convenience store, which was connected to the house.

She handed me a candle, some foil and a cardboard box. "Here, follow what I do," she said. She drew a circle on the cardboard and cut it out with a razor. Then she cut a small hole inside the circle and pushed a candle through it. She wrapped a long piece of foil under the candle until it covered the cardboard circle. I finally understood. It was a candleholder.

"That's so cool!" I shouted. Tatay told me to hush. I looked over to where he was standing and saw a long line of people. Then I realized they were trying to buy what I was trying to make.

*I*t turned out that every time a storm came around and the town lost electricity, people would run through the flooding streets to my grandfather's store to buy the candles that my grandfather and cousins would fashion for them. Putting the candles into their cardboard holders was hard work at first, but soon the process began to flow from my fingers and we became a two-person assembly line. I cut, I slid, I wrapped, and then I handed off. The finished product made me feel proud.

Mari and I laughed the whole time, playing with the fire on our desk in the stormy night, while our grandfather sold our works of art to his customers. When they had all gone, I made one for myself, lit it, and slid off my chair.

"Oh my gosh!" I screamed. Mari and Tatay laughed at me. The water had risen past my ankles, and I didn't understand why they weren't running to protect the house. Then it clicked. Everyone had been sitting on the chairs and couches waiting for the water to rise, and it had. It almost reached my knees now. I waded over to the living room, with the creatures of the earth— roaches, lizards, and the pet dog—swimming alongside me.

My family was sitting on desks, chairs, and couches above the rising water, chatting about politics and annoying neighbors. It felt strange to see everyone having a normal conversation while the house flooded. But I found beauty in it. In that living room was the calm of the storm.

I waded over to my youngest cousins who were playing with their Barbie dolls, and I combed their hair with my fingers. Every now and then the thunder would crackle and my two-year-old cousin would jump into my arms.

After a while, my cousins led me up the stairs and we all looked out the window. Before my eyes was the most breathtaking scene I'd ever witnessed. My view overlooked the whole town. In all the windows, I could see the candleholders I'd made. The lightning in the background lit the black sky. Rain blew onto my face and I didn't care. I saw the floodwater flowing downstream, and part of me wanted to jump in and let it take me anywhere it wanted to go.

Then, almost as quickly as it began, the storm quieted. As the lights went on, I saw every one of my candles being blown out, one by one.

I'd always judged my relatives and thought of them as poor, and even pitied them. But in that moment, I realized there were other ways to be rich—in family and in happiness.

Sitting up there on the windowsill—watching the flooded streets, knowing families were spending time together in their flooded homes—grounded me. It made me appreciate the precious time with my relatives, because I felt that they appreciated life itself. Suddenly, I desperately missed all the years I hadn't experienced with my cousins.

A week later, I was in my room packing, and my heart was breaking. I knew it'd be years before I'd see my relatives again because it's so expensive to travel to the Philippines. I'd miss their food, laughter, and love. I knew that my mom, dad, and brother loved me without a doubt, but this love was different. This was a community of love, and it made their lack of material things seem less important.

I rolled my suitcase down the stairs. Everyone was waiting there for me. All my aunts, uncles, and cousins kissed me and put their blessings on me. Finally, Tatay pulled me into a great big hug and gave me a kiss on my forehead. "Ingat. Mahal kita," he said. Take care. I love you.

I hugged him fiercely and kissed him goodbye. Then I ran out to the van and shut the door. I wasn't ashamed when my tears began falling.

Back in New York, I was more thankful for life and family. I became more focused on friendships and relationships. But while my parents spoke to my relatives on the phone every couple of weeks, I didn't keep in touch. My inability to speak Tagalog and their awkwardness with English made me feel shy about speaking to them.

As the months turned into years, I got caught up in my own affairs and my memories of the Philippines began to gather dust. Although I didn't completely forget about my relatives, they became distant to me. Life went on and I forgot about those emotions I'd had way back when.

But since both my grandfathers passed away recently, I've started thinking about my family again. I finally decided to set aside my guilt and get in contact with them.

I bought all seven of my cousins tote bags, multi-colored rhinestone bracelets, and Old Navy T-shirts. Then I e-mailed my cousin Michelle, who's now 23, married, and has a baby boy, to tell her the gifts were on the way.

Suddenly, I desperately missed all the years I hadn't experienced with my cousins.

With these gifts, I wanted to repay my cousins in some small way for the intangible gift they'd given me. I'd lacked that community of love they shared, and they let me experience it. So I wanted to give them what they lacked—these material items—even if they didn't need them.

After I e-mailed Michelle, I spent two weeks worrying about why she hadn't replied. Then one day I logged on and there was her response, waiting to be opened.

For a moment, I was afraid to read it. I worried it might be an angry message about how I hadn't kept in touch and how I assumed I could jump in and out of their lives whenever I pleased. I worried the connection might be gone. Then, in a rush of courage, I finally clicked "Open."

Michelle greeted me with a "Hello" and a "Thank you," saying I was kind to think of them. I was relieved when she explained that she wasn't very good with computers and that's why she hadn't replied right away.

But what made me smile from ear to ear, and reassured me that my community of love was still out there waiting for me, was the line right at the end:

"We love you and miss you. Hear from you soon."

Leneli was 16 when she wrote this story.
She later graduated from high school and attended college.

USA

MALAYSIA

Walter Moore

My Family Across the Ocean

By Anonymous

I looked at the date printed on the airline ticket in my hand: July 5. The day had come to leave Malaysia and move to New York to be reunited with my parents and brother. The plane was ready for boarding, but my feet were frozen inside my sneakers. The darkness outside was just right to go with my feelings.

All my relatives, friends, and teachers told me I was lucky I had the chance to move to the greatest country in the world. Even my loving godparents, who looked at me as if I was about to leave them forever, encouraged me to go. But no one ever asked if I wanted to go and leave behind everyone I cared about and everything I owned. It felt like my mouth was sealed with tape and I couldn't speak about my feelings. Suddenly, my tears came down like broken strings.

My mind was repeating every little moment I'd spent with

my cousins, friends, neighbors, and, most of all, my godparents, who'd raised me. I remembered having breakfast early in the morning with my godparents, and holding fresh meats and vegetables in the market while my godmother haggled with the vendors.

My biological parents lived in the U.S. with my younger brother, who was born a U.S. citizen, while they worked on getting green cards for me and for themselves. The only time I'd lived with them was when they returned to Malaysia for two years when I was 8.

I didn't recall much about them, but two scary memories remained in a corner of my brain: my mom hitting me with a hanger because I made mistakes on my homework, and my dad slapping me on the face for sweeping the floor incorrectly. Since then, I spoke to them on the phone about once a month, but we never talked about much besides school.

"I'll always be here when you need me," my godfather said. I hugged him tight and fell asleep slowly.

For 14 years of my life, my godparents were the ones who helped me grow in a happy family with lots of love. They were the ones who comforted me when I felt sad and brought me comfort when I needed it.

I felt how much they loved me even though I'm not their blood-related daughter. They held big birthday parties for me in gorgeous restaurants and invited a lot of relatives.

I was the youngest girl in the family and my godmother once told me that my godfather never hugged his other children, only me. When I did something wrong and my godmother scolded me, I'd lay my head on my godfather's shoulder so that he would defend me.

My godparents taught me how to read, how to write, and how to be happy. They said wise things to me, like, "Be generous to others so that in the future when you need help, they will help you," and, "No matter how hard something is, try before you give up, so that you won't regret anything."

If I was having a problem, I could always talk to my god-parents. One night in 6th grade, I was crying on my bed. My godfather came into my bedroom and saw me hiding inside my blanket like a little turtle. "What happened?" he asked.

"I was afraid of you and Mommy getting older while I grow bigger, and that you will pass away and leave me alone here," I sobbed. "Nobody will stay with me and sleep next to me when I have a nightmare."

"Don't worry my girl, you'll be all right," he said. "I'll always be here when you need me. Don't think too much." After that, I felt a little safer. I hugged him tight and fell asleep slowly.

I knew one day I would go to live with my parents in the U.S., but they'd been saying that for so many years I don't think I really believed it, until the day actually came when I had to start my new life on the other side of the planet.

When I saw my parents behind the glass wall at the airport, I felt like I was meeting strangers. That feeling didn't go away. From the moment I arrived, my parents treated me like I was an adult. They expected me to clean the house and take care of my 10-year-old brother because I'm older. They never sat with me and asked how I felt to be in New York with them, or told me anything about the city.

Soon I found out that my father ran a small business that delivered clothing to stores in Manhattan. What shocked me was the name of his company: It was named after my brother, and him only. That made me feel like even more of an outsider in my family.

I felt like a mute person who couldn't tell them I needed attention. One night my father saw me crying on the phone with my godmother. Later he asked me if I liked New York.

But when I sobbed and started with, "I..." he stopped me, saying, "You'll love living in New York after a year and you'll forget about Malaysia." I think he wanted to convince me—and maybe himself—that I'd be happy here eventually.

Things weren't any better with my mother. One of my aunts in New York told me my mom had missed me a lot when I was gone. But my mom didn't show it. She gave all her attention to my brother, buying him things and always asking him if he felt good or tired. I think she got used to giving all her love to him when I wasn't there, and she didn't realize she'd forgotten about me.

By my third month in the U.S., I felt that nothing was going well in my new life. I decided the best way to improve things was to focus on school. I had promised my godparents that I would study hard and make them proud.

I also wanted show my parents I could do well. My father always laughed at my English and praised my brother, who was born here, for his "perfect" English. I told myself if I showed effort and determination, I would get some positive attention from my parents. I began to stay up late at night, working on homework and projects so I could get them just right.

I've tried to become the kind of daughter my parents are looking for. But after three years, we are still like strangers.

My plan worked at first. When I got good grades on all of my subjects in my first term of school, my parents started using me as an example for my brother, telling him that he should study hard like I did. Every marking period when I got my report card, I felt proud.

But after a few months, my parents began to expect more from me. I had 90-plus grades in all my subjects, but they weren't satisfied because I didn't make 100. They also expected me to help my brother with his work. And if he did badly, they blamed me.

One night I was cleaning up after dinner when my dad asked my brother to show him the English test he'd just gotten back. When my dad saw the failing grade, he yelled, "How the hell did you get this grade? Didn't your sister review your homework and notes with you?"

He called me over and asked me to explain the low grade. I hadn't finished my explanation when he slapped me on my left cheek. His eyes turned mad, and he slapped me again.

All I felt was numbness. It reminded me of him hitting me when I was little. My dad hates his children to cry in front of him while he's giving us "advice." But I couldn't help it. I cried not only because he slapped me, but also because he didn't trust me.

I knew not to talk back to him, though. Instead, I responded inside my heart. "I didn't do anything wrong," I thought. "I followed your instructions and reviewed all the homework and notes with my brother. Why should I get blamed?"

I wished my godparents were there to answer those questions or listen to me. I spoke to them on the phone every weekend, but I felt I couldn't tell them how bad my situation was. They were expecting everything to be wonderful for me here, and I didn't want them to be worried or disappointed.

I've tried to become the kind of daughter my parents are looking for. I listen to them and I respect them as my parents. I've tried to change the way I get mad easily and immediately show my unhappy face to people. I've tried not to depend on others so much, and to be more proactive in learning new things like cooking.

But after three years, my parents and I are still like strangers. They don't hit me anymore, but they still yell when they're in a bad mood, and sometimes they just ignore me, which makes me feel even worse. When they do make an effort, I don't trust it because it never lasts longer than a week. Mom might cook me my favorite food and take me shopping, but then she ignores me or curses at me again.

For now, I'm just waiting to get out of the house. I don't want to talk to my parents about it because I don't think it will help. They never listen to me.

Luckily, my brother always stands by my side. When I feel bad about how my parents treat me I can talk to him, and sometimes he'll defend me when my mom is blaming things on me. Once, when my mom bought him some chocolate candies and nothing for me, he saved some and gave them to me when she wasn't around. And he spends all his allowance just to get me my birthday present. So even though I'm jealous of how well my mom treats him, I'm glad I have him as my brother.

I'm also glad I came to New York, because it gave me the chance for a better education, and to meet people from all over the world and learn about their cultures. But I still plan to move back to Malaysia and live near my godparents after I graduate from college. One day I hope to have my own children, and my godparents will be grandparents to them, just as they were parents to me. I want to take care of my godparents as they get old. I want to be near them to recall the wonderful memories of my childhood, and to create new happy memories together.

The author was 18 when she wrote this story.

Chapter 3:
Culture Clashes

Justin Riley

My Chinese Family—
Not Like TV

By Yuh-Yng Lee

I'm Chinese and I came to America from Taiwan when I was 9 years old. When I arrived I had great hope for my new life in America. All I wanted was to be a typical American kid with a typical American family.

During the early years of my new life, I used to love watching all those good old American family shows on TV. I envied the love that was so evident in those families. I envied their closeness. The parents were always so supportive. If kids didn't do well in something they'd tell them, "It's OK; I know you did your best." They'd give them confidence.

When their kids wanted to do something, these parents would never hold them back. They'd encourage them. And if their kids had a problem—any problem at all—they could just go to mommy or daddy and talk about it. Then the problem would be resolved and everyone was happy.

For a long time I thought all American families were like that. And I thought that's the way all families should be. I used to wonder why my family wasn't. My parents never told me they loved me. They never hugged or kissed me like the parents on TV.

I thought they must not love me. They were always busy. They didn't really spend time with my sister and me. Sure, we ate, watched TV, and went shopping together, but I wanted us to be close emotionally. I needed that. I wanted the heart-to-heart talks. I wanted to be able to talk to my parents about anything.

But our relationship is not like that at all. Chinese parents don't really show affection that way. I think part of the reason is discipline. They believe in strict discipline. They'll even hit their kids to keep them in line. (You never see parents on American TV hitting their kids. They always talk to them gently.)

I believe in discipline. With good discipline you can keep your child away from drugs and crime. But when kids get overly disciplined by parents, they become afraid of them. If you're afraid of your own parents, how can you go to them and tell them things? Anything you say might get you punished. For a while, that was the case with me.

When I did something wrong, my parents yelled at me. Even when I brought home a 100 on a test, my dad would ask me, "Why didn't you get a 101?" How about "That's great!" for a change, or "I'm so proud of you"? All I ever get is "Do better. Look at this kid in the paper—he has a 99 average and he won first prize in the national science fair." I don't feel good about myself after that.

Chinese newspapers like to do profiles of overachievers in school. Every time my father sees one, he cuts it out and makes me read it. After I finish, he gives me a lecture about how I should be more like that. Then he sticks the article on the refrigerator to remind me. My parents don't mean for it to happen, but all they do is bring down my self-esteem. They push me so I'll do better, but the effect is the total opposite.

That's another reason why I always envied the kids on TV. They can have fun. They don't have to stay home and study their heads off. Their parents stress education, but not like Chinese parents.

The Chinese see education as the key to a good future and greater opportunities. That's the main reason many Chinese parents come to America. My parents had comfortable jobs in Taiwan and made a decent living. When they came here, they had to take jobs waiting tables and doing other manual work. They gave up good lives for me, and I often feel guilty for not living up to their expectations.

My parents gave up good lives for me, and I often feel guilty for not living up to their expectations.

All the same, sometimes when I'm home studying so I can get a good grade on tomorrow's exam while my friends are out partying and enjoying their youth, I resent my parents. Typical American teens always seem able to go out and have a ball. They live for the moment and don't seem to worry about the future.

I've always thought that I got cheated out of my childhood. It seems as if my life is always filled with books, academic worries, grades, and my parents' dissatisfaction. Sometimes I wish I could be a typical American teen and just throw these worries away. I get so fed up that I want to say, "To hell with what my parents think."

That's easier said than done, though. Chinese kids are taught to respect and obey their elders. Despite strong American influences, I definitely have Chinese values. Every Chinese kid wants their parents' approval. I value my parents' words and want them to be proud of me.

Chinese kids have to do well in school. I understand that. If you do well, you have a future, and the future is very important. But I also want to enjoy the present. If only I weren't caught between these two cultures.

Yuh-Yng was 17 when she wrote this story. She went on to attend New York University and later became an accountant.

Can I Have Both?

By Fanny Brito

"Look, this is a platano," said Enrique, an old classmate I ran into at a supermarket in the Dominican Republic last spring break.

"Umm...I know what a platano is. I happen to eat them all the time back in New York," I said. I felt offended, but it wasn't the first time I'd been treated like a tourist in my own country.

When I'm in the Dominican Republic, I feel like I belong there. Yet other Dominicans see me differently because I've lived in America. Though it bothers me, I'm starting to realize that it's true: being American as well as Dominican makes me different.

I've lived most of my life—about 11 of my 17 years—in the Dominican Republic. However, I was born in New York, and that's where I live now. When I went back to the D.R. last April, I was anxious and happy to see my old friends and family. I got out of the airplane and took slow steps, immediately closing my eyes to the shining sun. The moment I felt that familiar breeze of warm, humid air in my face, I knew I was home.

My parents have been dragging me back and forth between the two countries since I can remember. They'd spend one year working really hard in New York; then they'd move back to the Dominican Republic and try to make a living there by buying property—houses, cars, and land—and renting them out.

I was happy when, in the 4th grade, we moved back to the Dominican Republic to stay for several years. Instead of sharing a room with my parents in New York, I had my own bedroom in the D.R.. I liked being able to go outside and play with my friends in our yard.

In New York my parents worked long hours, but in the D.R. they were home much more, and I spent more time with them. Unlike in New York, we ate most meals together.

I liked having my mom with me. She taught me "chores every woman should know," like how to iron, cook, and clean. My dad taught me how to wash his car and change the tires so that when I'm old enough to have my own car, I won't need any man to help me. (Though I think he just wanted somebody to wash his car for him.)

My Dominican family gave me special treatment, because with more money comes a higher social status.

While I felt I was living a typical Dominican kid's life in a typical Dominican family, some of my relatives acted like I was different because I'd lived in the United States. At the time, I didn't understand it.

Occasionally some of my cousins would act as if I had nothing in common with them. They asked me questions to test my "Dominican abilities": did I know how to cook traditional food and wash clothes? They were surprised to discover my mother had taught me these things that were expected of girls my age in the D.R..

Sometimes they'd go into one of the bedrooms and not invite

me to go with them. I tried to ignore them, but I felt left out. They also acted very defensive around me, as if they assumed I thought I was better than them, which I didn't.

Other people in the D.R. I'd known my whole life treated me like a tourist. They called me *gringa* or *la Americana*. My aunts and uncles referred to me, like they did to my parents, in a more formal way than to the rest of the family: they used *usted* rather than *tu*.

I didn't feel like I deserved special treatment, and it somehow built a barrier between us. I wasn't able to joke around with them as I did with my other uncles and aunts back in New York.

I think they treated me this way because I'm "American," which in the D.R. usually means you have more money, and with more money comes a higher social status. Many people said we were wealthy.

It's true that even though we lived uncomfortably when we lived in New York, in the D.R. my family had a car and a nice house. The house had three full-size bedrooms, each with a big closet; one bathroom; two dining rooms; a living room; a big kitchen; and two big *galerias*. (A *galeria* is like a screened-in porch, only with bars around it.) We had a back yard and front yard with mango, orange, and lemon trees that my dad planted to remind himself of how he grew up, growing his own food.

That's more than most families have in the D.R.. Most of my relatives there don't have cars, and they have smaller houses in not-so-good neighborhoods. They have enough for their basic necessities and sometimes enough to go out to dinner or to the movies, but those things are luxuries. Most of them work in textile factories and dress in a simple way, wearing inexpensive clothes.

Still, what my relatives and friends in the D.R. didn't see was my family's cramped lifestyle in New York and my parents' hard work and long hours. This is because Dominicans who've never come to New York only see the end results achieved by the people who go to New York to work. They have no idea how hard it is for uneducated Dominican immigrants—who often work 12 hours a day in a hot, unsafe factory in New York—to make even a lame amount of money. My parents and many of my relatives worked this way when they first arrived. And because rent in New York is so expensive, "home" is often just a small bedroom in a relative's house.

Each time my family moved back to New York, my parents would try to buy a small corner convenience store and worked 12-hour days, seven days a week. We'd live in a small apartment with my aunt, her husband, and her two teenage kids; my parents and I shared a small room. Most of the time, my mother and father were tired and cranky when they got home, complaining about things and fighting with me because I misbehaved or didn't clean my side of the room.

Still, living like that was worth it because making it in the Dominican Republic is far harder. My parents used to tell me about how bad their circumstances were before they came to New York. Though they worked many hours, they were only able to afford their everyday needs; they were never able to save money.

More than I want to admit, my family's hard work in New York has made me la Americana.

My father was in the Dominican army for a few years. He drove a truck, and then he and my mother managed to buy a grocery store there. When they decided to come to the U.S. the first time, they had to sell their house to pay for the plane tickets and the paperwork. But working hard in the United States paid off for them. They saved money. When they came back to the D.R., they could buy things.

To those who live and work only in the D.R., things seem very expensive. But when you work in New York and take dollars to the D.R., it's easy to feel rich. For example, a haircut in a salon there cost me 60 pesos, or about $3; in New York a haircut usually costs me $25.

My family is a vivid example of how hard work in New York can take you a long way. But more than I want to admit, my family's hard work in New York has made me *la Americana* in some ways. For one thing, as an American citizen I have the opportunity to choose between the U.S. and the D.R., unlike my relatives in the D.R. who have to stay there. And part of me feels more comfortable in the U.S.

When I was in the 9th grade and we'd been living in the D.R. for five years straight, my parents decided we were moving back to New York. I was glad. My life in the D.R. had started to feel limited because young people there don't have the same expectations and opportunities I'd been raised with. Like many American families, my parents expect me to go to school, start a career, and then form a family.

Although things are changing, young people in the D.R. are expected to marry and form a family when they are young (early 20's), and most women stay home and take care of the children. It's also difficult to go to college in the D.R. because it's extremely expensive and there's very little help available for tuition. Only middle class people who live in cities are expected to go to college and have careers.

When I thought about what I wanted for my future, I realized how much I wanted something different from what my family has in the D.R.. I plan to finish my senior year of high school in New York, then go to college in the U.S. Like my parents, I see more opportunities here than in the D.R.. My future is in the U.S.

I'm glad that New York adopted us (and many other immigrants) and gives us many opportunities that we wouldn't have in the D.R.. I love this city, its people, its controversies, its opportunities. But I also feel grateful that my parents raised me in two places.

Spending most of my childhood in the D.R., I was able to learn my home country's values and culture. I like how people in the D.R. are friendly and funny, and more laid back than people in New York. In New York, you don't pass by a person's house and say hi to them if you don't know them, while in the D.R., that's expected. There's life in the streets in the Dominican Republic: people playing dominos, hanging out, talking. Days feel longer, since you have time to visit people at their houses and drink a cup of coffee while you're sitting down, something I've never done in New York.

Sometimes I really miss that other life.

Fanny was 17 when she wrote this story.

YC Art Dept.

Not My Father's Daughter

By Sarvenaz Ezzati

In July I got a letter in an airmail envelope with Islamic stamps and Farsi writing on it. I immediately recognized that it was from Iran, the country I fled with my mother nine years ago, when I was 8. The sender was my father. Even though I haven't seen him in more than seven years, I'm still afraid of him.

I've always felt that if my father wanted to he could take me back to Iran. And since a girl belongs to her father like property there, he would have the right to marry me off to someone of his choice and get a dowry in exchange. Many times he threatened my mother that he would kidnap me and take me back to Iran. This caused me to be very wary of all Iranians, because I know how persuasive my father can be. If he said the right words, he could get anyone to help him.

When we first came to this country and socialized with other

Iranian families, adults would casually ask me questions about my mother and myself, and then convey the information back to my father. We soon learned to avoid other Iranians—especially Iranian men.

Then one day last summer, I heard two Iranian men on the train speaking Farsi, fluently and eloquently. I became very emotional and depressed. I realized how much of my Iranian culture and heritage I had given up because I was trying to protect myself from my father. I will probably never again dance the special Persian dances I once loved. Or attend festive parties like the ones I remember going to with my parents in Iran, where all generations celebrated together, guests were treated like royalty, and everyone shared huge plates of delicious meat stews and rice. For a moment, these happy memories allowed me to forget the dark side of thoughts about my father and my country.

I realized how much of my Iranian heritage I had given up because I was trying to protect myself from my father.

Iran is now a place I fear and would never go back to voluntarily. It's a very religious and old-fashioned country. Women are supposed to be passive and quiet, and they are considered the weaker sex, mentally and physically. When the Ayatollah Khomeini seized power in 1979, overthrowing the Shah of Iran, he wanted to lead the country with the laws of the Qur'an, the Islamic holy book.

Through his own personal translations of the Islamic laws, Khomeini took the rights of women away, forcing them again to wear black chadors (a veil that covers the entire body), denying them educational opportunities (the majority of Iranian women were illiterate), and telling Iranian men that knowledge for a woman was dangerous because women are not capable of working and making decisions for themselves.

The radical change from the Shah, who was very modern in his ideas about women's roles, to the repressive Ayatollah

Khomeini literally happened overnight. One morning my mother woke up and realized she was the property of my father and that all her rights had been taken away. She also knew that any educational opportunities I would have had under the Shah were now nonexistent. We were like free birds suddenly trapped in a cage of religious oppression and darkness.

As the country became more oppressive, my mother's life there became unbearable. My mother speaks five different languages, was a straight-A student in high school, and upon graduation at the age of 18, began teaching Air Force pilots how to speak, read, and write English. But she never went to college because her father felt she should be married and that college for a girl was a waste of money.

When my mother married my father, she loved him and looked forward to a happily-ever-after relationship despite warning signals, like the other girlfriends he flaunted. It wasn't long after they were married that my father started to lie to my mother and sleep around. When he was angry, he beat her.

My father's approach to running his business was no better than his approach to marriage. Eventually, dishonest business dealings landed him in jail. Since my mother had helped out in his business, she knew the authorities were preparing to come after her, too. This hastened her decision to flee the country.

Here in the U.S., I've been raised to think of myself as equal to men and to make decisions for myself. I fear going back to Iran because I would not be able to go to college, have a career of my own, or even wear what clothing I like. I know that I could never live like the many Iranian women who take orders from their husbands and are financially and socially dependent. If a woman is not married in Iran, or if she is divorced, she is considered rotten, like spoiled milk. I could never survive in such an oppressive environment.

Young women in this country take for granted that they can go to college, dress how they please, and choose for themselves who they will marry. I, on the other hand, am always afraid that I will lose my opportunities to get an education and start my own career. I fear that I will end up married to a man like my father.

When I received my father's letter, my feelings of fear mixed with distrust. Because of the person he is, I know that even a letter that says nice things may contain danger.

Here in the U.S., I've been raised to think of myself as equal to men and to make decisions for myself.

My mother and I left Iran after struggling for four years to get green cards. My father promised to join us in the United States once he took care of his business. (Even after everything he did to her, my mother was willing to give him another chance.) But after three years he told my mother that he wanted us to return to Iran instead.

His reason was that he didn't want to give up his $1 million business in Iran. He told us that the situation for women in Iran had improved. But he was lying—Iranian women still had no rights. This didn't seem to bother him. He just didn't want to give up his business. I felt abandoned because his money meant more to him than I did.

I wasn't really surprised to get a letter from my father because occasionally he sends me something saying that he still thinks about me. He sometimes sends me gifts from Iran, telling me he cares for me, and that any unhappiness I feel is because of my mother. His gifts always feel like bribes to turn me against my mother. Instead, my trust in him lessens with every gift.

But there was something in this letter that I never expected. My father said that it was his duty as a father to pay for my college education—a bill my mother can't pay alone.

Now I feel that I'm being bribed once again, but the stakes are higher. He's willing to pay for my entire college education. This could be the chance of a lifetime. Since my grades are average, it's not very likely that I can get a full scholarship or grant. And it would be a big luxury if I could graduate college without a loan to pay back afterwards. With the money my mother would save, she could afford to send me abroad to study in London or Paris, and give me extra spending money.

Yet I feel like I'm being bought, and that if I accept the offer I would be letting my father off the hook. For the price of my college education, my father would want forgiveness and a second chance to be the father he never was.

I have to make my decision soon and it isn't an easy one, not like winning Lotto, where someone hands me a big fat check with no strings attached. After all, why would he make this offer without expecting me to allow him into my life again? If he pays, he could expect me to play the role of dutiful daughter. And, if I accept, I'll be committed to a relationship with him that I might not be ready for.

Sarvenaz was 17 when she wrote this story. She graduated from high school and college and became a school teacher.

Froylan Garcia

Score One for Team Spirit

By Philippe Sainvil

In my country, Haiti, soccer is the number one sport. I don't remember the exact age I was when I started playing, but by the time I was 7, I was pretty good. Every time I stepped on a soccer field, when I smelled the grass or when I kicked the ball, I got a feeling of liberation. It was like all the problems—all the talking, all the drama that I had in my life—vanished, and a new door for fun and joy opened.

I used to play with my three brothers, my cousin, and other friends from the neighborhood. We all shared the same language, signals, and style of playing. For example, to ask for a pass, you'd stick your tongue out and shake it. To ask for a long pass you'd say, "Male" (meaning "I'm going for it"). We barely did high or long passes; instead we mostly did footwork and kept the ball on the grass, where we'd have more control over it. These tricks made our games exciting and fast-paced.

I had to give up those games when I moved to New York. When I left Haiti, I thought I'd be attending a high school just like in the movies, with white American students. But I wound up attending an immigrant school, so there were no native-born Americans at all. Instead, there were kids from all around the world.

I liked the fact that I was able to explore different cultures all in the same place. That was amazing, especially during Culture Day. On Culture Day we had flags and colors everywhere, and students brought food, juice, candy, or anything from their native land to share with others. Every country put their food out in one or two classrooms, and all the students and school staff visited and ate in every room. I never got to taste everything, but from what I tasted I was blown away, especially by the Asian foods.

Most of the time, though, the school was divided. One lunch period, during my first week at school, I sat next to some Middle Eastern students. After about 45 seconds, a Haitian student came up to me and said, "Aren't you Haitian?"

I said, "Yeah."

"Then why are you sitting with the Arab people? Come sit with us," he said in Creole (the language of Haiti).

I did not fully understand why he said that, but I just got up and followed his advice. I was new to the school and I was a little lost. I figured he had been there longer, so he knew better.

After that, I noticed that the whole cafeteria was divided by race or nationality. Haitians had lunch with Haitians, Eastern Europeans with Eastern Europeans, Africans with Africans, Spanish speakers with Spanish speakers, and so it went. Besides this, discrimination and insults between the different groups were common. Walking through the hallways, you could hear people talk crap about other races for no justifiable reason, stuff like:

"These European people dress stupidly."

"Africans sound like monkeys."

"Mexicans are short and ugly."

Fortunately, we did have one big thing in common. Almost everyone in the school loved soccer, since it was popular in all of our native countries. A group of us who wanted to play got together and begged our principal at least to try to get us into a league. But even though we had a basketball team that got jerseys, balls, and everything they needed, he told us he did not have enough money to fund a soccer team.

After I'd been in the school a year, we moved as a school to a new building that we shared with other high schools. (We had one floor to ourselves.) The schools in this building combined to form one soccer team, and the previous year that team had had the worst record in the local soccer league. They were at the bottom of the table with no draws and no wins, only losses.

As soon as we arrived at our new building, all of us in the international high school who wanted to play soccer sent our medical sheets and permission slips to the athletic director. We were all excited and confident. When the time came for us to meet the coach so we could talk about the team and ask questions, we arrived at the school 30 minutes early. The coach was amazed at how many of us made the trip. "We're going to have a good season," he said.

Practice started. Twenty out of 25 players on the team were from the international high school. But even though we were enthusiastic, the first days of practice turned out badly, because the way we were divided at school carried over to the soccer field.

Most of us kept passing the ball only to players from our own country. We all knew that we should pass the ball to any teammates who were open, no matter what their nationality. But we just didn't do it. To be honest, I was as bad as anyone. If I had the ball I tended to pass it to a Haitian, even if there were three other players open in a better situation.

After about a week, we had a team meeting. It was a sunny afternoon before we started practice and the coach brought us all together in the middle of the pitch. We were all wondering what it was about.

He started by saying, "I've seen you practicing and I can tell that you are all talented players." We kept listening as he continued, "But we lack some things as a team, and these qualities that we lack are essential to success."

He told us that if we didn't play with sportsmanship, leadership, and teamwork, we would not just lose all season, we would no longer have a team. The school had had so many losses during previous seasons, he said, they were thinking about getting rid of the soccer team altogether. "Those who do not want to show teamwork will either be on the bench or off the team," he said finally.

At first, some of us got upset.

"Africans and Mexicans suck. I will not play with these dumb players…"

"I'm not playing with Russians; they are harassing me!"

But most of us stayed on the team and tried to change our way of playing. Because everyone was making the effort, it was easier than it would have been otherwise. We started to work together and look out for one another. Everyone began passing the ball around to anyone on the team, and soon we were playing real soccer with a lot of passing. Little by little, our passion for soccer proved stronger than our prejudice and division.

I noticed that the whole cafeteria was divided by race or nationality.

At last the season began. From the beginning, we were winning games with scores of 13-0 or 7-2. Our effort to come together was paying off, not only because of the winning scores, but because we were having more fun than we would ever have imagined.

But when it came time to face the team that was our league's defending champion, everyone knew that it wouldn't be easy. We were all nervous. It was a home game for us and it was the first time we'd had that many spectators—both students and school staff—coming to watch us play. Also, because we had turned the team around so much already, we were making news: There was a *New York Daily News* reporter watching the game and taking pictures.

I will never forget that special September afternoon. We won the game 3-2, and I scored the first two goals. This was a huge victory and the *Daily News* reporter interviewed me and some other players. We made it to the newspaper, where we were featured in a three-page article with lots of photos. "Infusion of Immigrants Transforms Last-Place Lafayette," read the headline.

We had one big thing in common: Almost everyone in the school loved soccer.

After that we no longer believed that we could go far, we knew it. The newspaper article was pasted all over our building, and they put up a big poster of the soccer team in the school weight room. We felt important and appreciated, like our hard work was taken seriously. We were proud of ourselves.

After all the fun we'd had as a team, we became pretty close. We began to hang out together, even outside of practice. We'd joke together and say, "What's up," or "Hey," every time we saw each other.

Some of us ended up being good friends, and still are now. I made friends with a Russian and an African teammate. We still don't sit together in the cafeteria during lunch period, but it's not because we're enemies. I think it's because we've been doing things this way for so long that it's become a habit and it's hard to break.

Playing soccer with Haitians is still fun to me, but when you play with other folks you get to try out different styles of soccer. You also feel more professional, like the pro players on TV who have teammates from all around the world. Each player has a unique style and skill.

To this day, I get the very same feeling of liberation when I play soccer that I used to get as a kid back in Haiti. But now, I see how soccer can liberate us even from our divisions.

Philippe was 16 when he wrote this story.

John Jones

University of Kitchen?

By Orubba Almansouri

"We're halfway through the summer. Are we going to New York or what?" I asked my older sister Yasmin. She had come to visit us at our house back in my country, Yemen. We were in the room we'd shared until she got married and moved away.

"Do you really want to go?" she replied, opening the Kit Kat bar she had in her hand.

"Yes and no," I answered as I lay down on my bed. "I want to stay here for you and all our extended family, but I also want to see Dad and New York City."

"What's the rush, then? It's not like you're going to school when you get there," she said.

In my family, most men believe that the best place for a woman is in the house and the best job for us women is to cook, clean, and raise a family. Many girls in my family—including

Yasmin—stop going to school before they reach high school, and none have gone to college. Girls live with their families until they are 15 or a little older, and then it's time to say goodbye to being single and hello to marriage.

My religion, Islam, is not against girls being educated. In fact our Prophet Mohammed, may peace be upon him, said that we should seek education even if we have to go to China for it. The problem isn't my culture either, since many Yemeni girls are educated and have jobs. Where my family's tradition came from, I don't know. But so far, no one has broken it.

There is always a question mark over my future.

I never imagined my destiny would be any different. In my country I was an excellent student and teachers loved me. In 7th grade, I was first in my class. They put my name in big letters on a piece of paper and hung it up in the main hallway. I felt so proud of myself.

I didn't mind leaving school at any time, though, because I knew the path girls in my family followed and I didn't expect anything else. When we came to the United States the first time (when I was 5—we stayed for a few years), my older sisters were teenagers and they didn't get a chance to go to school, even though they really wanted to go and learn English. So when I was 14 years old and I heard that we were moving back to the U.S., I figured I wouldn't be going to school anymore.

Then we got to New York, and my dad announced he was planning to enroll my sister Lebeya and me in school. I was surprised. From what I used to see on TV, American high schools were another planet compared to schools in Yemen. I wasn't used to going to school with boys, or talking to them. In fact, I was a little worried: I'd heard that many Yemeni students who go to American high schools start to do what the other kids are doing, like having relationships and even drinking, neither of which is allowed by my religion. I'd expected my dad would want to keep my sister and me away from this environment. (My mom wants us to be educated, as she never had the chance to be, but like most Yemeni women she follows her husband's decisions.)

But my dad was determined. When my oldest sisters didn't go to school in New York, that affected their lives and his. They couldn't go out alone because they didn't understand English and couldn't communicate. My dad had to translate for them at doctors' appointments. When we moved to New York, he said putting my sister and me in school would help us become independent so we could help ourselves when necessary.

For my part, I decided that since I had the chance to go to school, I would definitely take it. Today my sisters are both married and have children sweet as honey, but they still wish they had gone to school here and learned to speak English. I saw from my sisters' experience that education was the best thing for me, and I felt that going to school might be fun and a way to get out of the house. I had no idea what it would come to mean to me.

While we were getting records and report cards sent from Yemen to New York so my sister and I could enroll here, the men in my extended family started telling my dad that we would get ourselves into trouble and hurt the family's reputation. They thought that high school in America would Americanize us, causing us to drop the traditions we'd been learning our entire lives and pick up others.

One day my dad was on the phone with one of my cousins and I heard some of my dad's replies. (It's not my fault he thought that I was sleeping when I wasn't.) They went like this:

"They are my daughters and I have raised them right. I know what is good for them."

"It's none of your business."

"I don't care what they say, I have listened to you guys once and I won't make that mistake again."

After I heard that, I was saying to myself, "Way to go, Dad!" I saw my father as someone who is ready to make a change and someone who really cares about his daughters' education; I saw him in a way that made me feel proud to be the daughter of Ali Almansouri. I knew that my dad had put all his trust in us, and this made me want to be on my best behavior.

My first day at Brooklyn International High School was scary because I was starting 9th grade at the end of September and I was the new girl. I felt lonely at first, but luckily my English was OK from living here as a kid. By second period I'd talked to two Hispanic girls and we became friends. My teachers were so nice to me; they helped me when I needed help and they always asked me how I was doing. I began to love school once again. I worked hard and got excellent grades. My classmates started telling me, "You're so smart."

I don't believe that I'm as smart as they say, but I do believe that I am clever. Because I did well, ideas of actually graduating started coming into

After that, I saw my father as someone who really cares about his daughters' education.

my head. My love for school grew, especially when I learned new things, went on trips, or met new friends.

"You know that I will be the first girl from our family to actually go to college," I said one day to my sisters and a group of other girls, while we were sitting together talking.

"Yeah, and you'll go to the University of Kitchen," my younger cousin said.

"And earn your cooking degree," my sister added.

Then they all started laughing, including me. "You'll see, when I become the first Almansouri girl to go to college and break the 'girls don't go to college' rule," I said. "You'll see what I will do."

The truth is, though, that there is always a question mark over my future. In spite of the things I overheard my dad say on the phone, his decisions about my future are not all made yet. My dad doesn't really follow up on my schoolwork, and when opportunities come up—like leadership programs or after school activities—it's not easily that he lets me participate.

I think that even though he put me in school, sometimes he still thinks the way other men in my family do. This worries me, because it makes me think he may not allow me to finish the path that he let me start. However, if I give him a great speech about why he should let me do some extracurricular thing, and if I'm persistent, he usually gives in. I think that when I put it in his head that I can benefit a lot from these things, he sees it, and that gives me hope for the future.

My being allowed to finish high school and go to college depends on two people: Dad and me. I will never disobey him because he is everything to me. My basic hope is that we don't go back to Yemen before I graduate from high school. Then, if my dad lets me, I'd prefer to put off marriage until I am settled in college.

What will actually happen, I don't know. My dad hasn't told me what he's thinking. Even though I hate not knowing what's going to be next, in another way I don't want the topic to come up yet. I'm afraid of the answer I'll get, in case it's a "no." Anyway, as they say, you have to walk up the ladder step by step or you'll fall down.

When I'm feeling hopeful, I think my dad will let me go to college. I want to attend a good college like Columbia University, major in English or journalism, and also study biology. I see my future as a finish line with red and white stripes, and I see myself crossing the line, then getting my prize—in other words, working in a career and feeling true power and independence. I also want to feel useful to the world and to people around me. I want to learn more and be an educated person.

Sometimes, though, I feel that everything I do is for no reason and that I will never be able to go to college or even finish high school. I worry that if I do graduate from high school, my dad will say, "I already let you finish high school and we don't have women who go to college in this family." I worry about the pressure that will be on him if he does let me go to college. Our family made such a big deal about us going to high school, I can't imagine what they would say about college.

When I hear things from my family like, "Girls your age are getting married and soon it will be your turn," those comments are like rockets landing in my ears. I find a place to be alone and think to myself, "All this hard work, these top grades, these compliments, for what? For me to remember when I'm seasoning the soup. Why did they put me in the race when I had no interest in participating? They put the idea in my head, made me like it and actually work toward something—all so that when I reach the finish line they'll tell me I can't cross it."

I imagine watching others cross the line without me, and put myself down for all the time I spent dreaming of things I want to accomplish. "Maybe it's not time, Orubba," I think. "Maybe the girl that will break your family's record hasn't been born yet."

> *I think to myself, "All this hard work, these top grades, for what? For me to remember when I'm seasoning the soup."*

With that I cry myself to sleep. Sometimes I even have nightmares about not finishing high school. A lot of people think that it's no big deal; I'll get married and my husband will give me everything I need. But that's not enough for me because I want my life to have different flavors and taste them all, not just repeat the same flavor over and over every day. I also want to feel that I'm prepared if something happens to my husband. How will I feed my children? I want to have a weapon in my hand and education is one weapon that never hurts anyone, but actually helps.

In Yemen, I always thought that going to college was a good thing for girls, but I didn't feel envious of the girls from other families who could go. Since I came to the U.S., though, I have been thinking more about my future. I want more out of life. Because I see college as a possibility for me, but not a sure thing, today I feel envious toward Yemeni girls who know they can go to college.

Sometimes I get mad that my family keeps on pushing boys to go to college, even though most of them don't have any interest, while some of us girls are ready to work for it and never get a chance. Other times, I tell myself that whatever education I end up with is better than nothing. I'm even a little afraid of going to college in case I fail. I'm torn between two things, but the tear is not straight down the middle. I'm happy that my obsession with success is greater than my worries.

Now I'm a junior, my grades are still excellent, and my desire to live my dream is greater than ever. I agree with some of my family's traditions, like girls not going out alone and not sleeping at anyone's house outside the family. But the education issue is too much. If they give all us girls a chance and support us, we can help our family reach higher than ever before. If I go to college, I'll open a path and be a role model for future generations of girls in the family, teaching them not to give up.

If my father's decision is for me to go to college, he will raise his head high and tell everyone who wanted to stand in my way that they were wrong; that he is happy and proud that he gave us a chance that a lot of parents in my family took away from their girls. I want him to be really pleased with what I accomplish.

Everything I become will be because of the trust he gave me. I will keep my religion and my traditions, but I will follow my dreams as long as I know that what I'm doing is right. I have no problem with cooking and cleaning, as long as it is a side order with my dream. But if my dad doesn't support my dream, then everything that I have planned for won't be. That's what causes me nightmares instead of dreams.

Orubba was 16 when she wrote this story.

Richard Johnson III

Too American for My Boyfriend

By Sue Chong

My boyfriend Kevin and I went out for a year and, during that time, we fought until we got sick of it. We fought about the stupid things all couples fight about, but the main thing that came between us was something that only immigrant couples would ever have to think about. We constantly argued about whether I was too Americanized.

Kevin and I both came to the U.S. from Korea five years ago. Although we had this in common, we had different points of view on everything.

He would ask me why I couldn't be like other Korean girls. If I were a "real" Korean girl, he felt, I would listen to him when he told me to do something, depend on him for most things, and think his way instead of my way. Whenever I didn't agree with him, we would have another fight.

To me, he was too Korean and too narrow-minded. He refused to accept any culture except his own, and he always thought his way was the only way.

I eat Korean food, I speak Korean, I have respect for my parents as Koreans have, I celebrate Korean holidays and traditional days. I even joined the Korean Club in school, so that I can keep my customs with my friends.

But since I came to this country, I have come to love certain customs from other cultures. For example, I see the way my Hispanic friends greet people with affection. They kiss and hug when they say "hello," and I love this. (In Korea, people are much more formal; they just shake hands and bow to each other out of respect.) So I started kissing my friends on the cheek, too.

I see my Hispanic friends greet people with affection, and I love this. I started kissing friends on the cheek, too.

Kevin didn't like this, and he told me so. He even asked me to stop it. I didn't want to, so I did it anyway, though not as much. Later on, he told me again not to kiss and hug other people. I asked him why, and he told me that he didn't like it and that other Koreans didn't act the way I did. He couldn't accept it.

Korean men like to tell their wives and girlfriends what to do. He would always tell me how to dress and how to act in front of others. He wanted me to stay next to him all the time. I would complain that I was not his little toy and that he couldn't just order me around.

When I would go against his wishes, Kevin would say, "Why are you so Americanized?" I didn't know how to respond to that. He said I must be ashamed of my country and my culture to act the way I did. I was shocked, and those words hurt me badly. I was not ashamed of my country or culture. I am proud of being Korean. I just want to accept other cultures, too.

I can't deny that I sometimes act like an American, trying to be more independent and outgoing than other Korean girls. But I still act like a Korean, too, in many ways; I am trying to balance two cultures. Through my boyfriend, I got a chance to think about who I really am. I realized that I am both a Korean and an American.

Sue was 17 when she wrote this story.

Justin Riley

Home Is Where the Hurt Is

By Zeena Bhattacharya

For the first 10 years of my life I lived with my grandparents in Calcutta, India. I didn't know my parents at all. Then, one spring afternoon, I came home from school and found my grandmother packing. "Are we going somewhere?" I asked. "Yes, to your parents, in Madras," she answered.

My parents had sent me to live with my grandparents when I was only a few days old. No one ever told me why. Nor did they tell me why we were going to see them now. Still, I had never been to Madras before and I was very excited about going to a new place.

I went to my grandfather and sat on his lap. "Is it true we are going to Madras?" I asked. Just for a moment, I thought I saw tears in his eyes. But he smiled and said, "Yes, I'm taking you there." Immediately I was reassured.

"Oh boy! I'm going to Madras—to M-A-D-R-A-S," I shouted and ran out to tell my friends. Not once did it occur to me that my life with my grandparents was about to end.

At first, I found Madras very beautiful. It was like a big vacation for me and my grandfather with the two strange people I had only known from pictures. But after a month, my grandfather left. I was heartbroken—of all the people in the world, I loved and trusted him the most. How could he leave me with these people I had known for only a month? But I tried to make the best of it.

I tried to do everything my parents asked me to. They never really talked to me—just ordered me to do things or not do things. Sometimes my mother would break into fits, shouting that I was such an obstacle in her life. My father also said I was a terrible burden. Soon their words turned into beatings.

My mother was very particular about how she kept her house. She would always remind me that if I weren't there it wouldn't be such a mess. Once she started hitting me because she had asked me to make the bed in a particular way. But I had done it another way. "What difference does it make?" I asked.

That made her even angrier. As soon as my father came home she told him that I was disobedient and had the nerve to talk back to her.

In India, it's the parents who never hit their children who are looked upon as neglectful.

He took off his belt and started hitting me with it. Then my mother grabbed me by the hair and started slapping me while my father continued with the belt.

Another time I had come into the drawing room not "properly dressed" for company. As soon as the guests left, my mother took a hot spatula from the stove and struck my cheek with it. My skin began to burn. I was so angry I said, "I hate it here, I want to go back."

When my father came in he started striking me with his belt again. "Do you think we want you here?" he asked. "Nobody wants you here. Such an impossible child—but I am going to fix you no matter what. I am going to fix you—I swear." And he kept on hitting me.

At school, my teacher saw the burn mark on my face and asked me what happened. After hesitating I told her. "Your poor mother," she said. "Do you know how much it hurt her to have done this to you? But what else can we do? You children don't learn unless we hit you."

Another girl in the class raised her hand and said, "My mother beats me with a ruler but it's only because she loves me." In India, it is considered "proper discipline" to hit a child. Over there, it's the parents who never hit their children who tend to be looked upon as neglectful.

Even in school we were beaten. Once, those of us who hadn't done our homework had to stand up and put out our palms so that the teacher could come around and strike us with her ruler. When she got to me she gave me this reproachful look and said, "You see, you still haven't learned, you bad girl," and gave me my punishment.

At home, my parents said I was the worst kind of child ever and needed a lot of discipline. "A bad child," they would tell their friends, "so disobedient."

The fact that I was a "bad child" was the answer to everything. My grandparents had sent me back because I was a "bad child." Everyone hated me because I was a bad girl. I started to believe I deserved to be treated this way.

When I was 12, my father was transferred to a job in the U.S. As a teenager in New York City, dealing with my parents became even harder. My friends would go to parties and movies and I would be stuck at home. Sometimes, when I did something they didn't like, my parents wouldn't even let me go to school.

I wasn't allowed to go out of the house alone until I started going to high school. And even then I had to get home by 4 p.m. One time I went to McDonald's after school to celebrate the birthday of one of my closest friends. I only stayed for about ten minutes, though, because I didn't want to get in trouble. I rushed home and got there by 4:20. My mother was waiting near the door and started slapping me as soon as I walked in.

When my father got home she told him to "ask her which guy was she f--king that she was an hour late." She said I had started to curse at her when she asked for an explanation. I was used to her exaggerating things and didn't even try to defend myself. I knew my father wouldn't wait to hear my side. And he didn't, he just

The fact that I was a "bad child" was the answer to everything.

started kicking me and swearing that he would fix me if it took his whole life. I just thought it was my fault. I shouldn't have gone with my friends in the first place.

My friends would invite me to go ice skating and to their parties. My parents would never let me go. After a while I just stopped trying to get permission and the invitations stopped coming. I used to get depressed because I believed no one liked me. My grades started dropping.

Once I tried to join an after school club. Since it was a writing club I thought that I could just take the work home with me. But when I found out there were meetings I had to attend, I dropped out. I explained to my teacher that I had to get home by 4 o'clock and that my parents called every day to make sure I was there. "And what would happen if you weren't?" he asked, "I would be in trouble," I answered, trying to say as little as possible.

The teacher wrote my parents a letter asking them to let me join the club, but they refused and my father slapped me. He was angry in a way I had never seen him before. How dare I complain to strangers about him?

Although I couldn't imagine telling an adult about what was happening to me, sometimes I would confide in my friends. "You should call the police," some said. But the thought of police coming to our house scared me. "Why don't you run away?" others suggested. Perhaps the worst thing I heard was: "Oh, you're exaggerating, it isn't so bad. Both of your parents are together. You are the only child. What are you complaining about? They're just overprotective."

Then one day, during another conversation with my teacher, I blurted out, "They hit me with a belt." At first I didn't think he was going to take me seriously. I thought he might say something like, "So what? I hit my kids with a belt, too." Instead he looked at me very seriously for a moment and then asked, "When was the last time they did that?"

I remembered what my friends had said about calling the police. And I was afraid he was going to do just that. "It's really nothing. I am the one who's bad, really," I said. I was remembering the grade school teacher who had labeled me a "bad child." I hated the way she had embarrassed me in front of the class, but I preferred that to having my parents reported to the police. I tried to explain to him that my parents believed hitting was the best way to discipline a child—that in India hitting a child was considered appropriate, even necessary.

"But with a belt?" my teacher asked. "I have two children; one is 18 and the other is 21. I have never hit them."

I just couldn't believe him. He must have forgotten. I didn't think it was possible to raise kids without ever hitting them.

"Well, you're not going to do anything, are you?" I asked nervously. Inside, I was thinking, "Oh, God, can't you just forget it?"

He explained to me that as a teacher he was required by law to "report" any child he suspected of being abused. The next day I was called to my guidance counselor's office. They told me that they wanted to call my parents.

That night I couldn't sleep. I just couldn't imagine how my parents would react if the school called. The counselor had asked me to describe how I thought my parents would react. All I could manage to say was, "They would be upset." But that was an understatement. I knew the result would be that they would take me back to India. I wished I could have taken back what I had said.

I tried to figure out how to convince my teacher and counselor that talking to my parents would do more harm than good. Finally they gave me a choice: they wouldn't call my parents if I agreed to go to counseling. Naturally, that's what I chose.

Once a week, I would go to my guidance counselor's office and she'd ask me what happened over the weekend, whether there had been any fights. Of course, it didn't change the situation, but talking about what was happening to me certainly helped me cope with it.

I began to understand that I didn't deserve to be treated that way.

One time I told my counselor how my mother had asked me to iron clothes in a certain order and I had done them in a different order. Before, I had thought I was being disobedient when I didn't do exactly what my parents said. But my counselor made me feel that it was bad enough that I had to iron everyone's clothes. She said that my mother had no right to get upset over the order I did it in.

The counselor made me see that other kids did things that were much worse and yet their parents didn't treat them half as badly as mine treated me. Soon I began to understand that I wasn't responsible for everything and I didn't deserve to be treated that way.

Just talking to my counselor made me feel better. I wondered why I hadn't been able to get to know her before. I guess I had thought that all adults would be like my parents. It was a big relief to find out that it wasn't true.

When summer vacation came I went back to India for a visit. One day I was walking through a park. Some families had built little homes there. One of the women who lived there was slapping a child so hard that I could hear it from down on the corner.

When I got closer I saw a skinny child, about 4 years old,

being beaten by his mother. He was naked from head to heels and his skin was red. Tears were rolling down his face but he wasn't shouting. It seemed to me that he was used to this.

Suddenly, on an impulse, I shouted, "Stop it!" The woman looked at me, astounded. "Do you want to kill him?" I asked more calmly.

When the mother finally recovered from the shock of my intrusion, she got very angry. "What's your problem, lady?" she managed to say. "He drank all the milk that we had for the week. Now his father is going to hit me."

Did parents have eternal control over their children? Why was anyone else powerless to stop them?

She kept shouting angrily at me: "It's none of your business what I do with my children." Just for spite, she struck the kid again. "What are you going to do about it?" she asked.

A good question. What was I going to do about it? Call the nearest child welfare agency? India didn't even have one, as far as I knew. Report the mother to the police? They would probably laugh at me. Get her therapy? Take him home with me when I didn't even have a home of my own?

I looked at the little boy's face again. The tears on his cheeks were almost dry. I turned away and started to leave. "Ha! These rich people think they can control everything," she called after me. "Hey woman, if you love my son so much why don't you take him with you?"

Suddenly I hated myself. Why did I have to butt in if I couldn't do anything in the end? Did parents have eternal control over their children? Why was anyone else powerless to stop them? Why didn't they have a child welfare agency here? And even if they did, would it solve the problem? In the U.S., we still have cases of kids being killed by abusive parents. I realized I had to learn more about child abuse and what to do about it.

When I returned to New York, I decided that no matter what, I was going to help myself and others in my situation. I decided I wanted to do a research project on child abuse for a national science competition. In order to do that I would have to stay at school till 6 p.m. once a week. My parents still expected me home by 4 p.m. every day, but I applied to do the project anyway. I was determined that they weren't going to stop me.

My project proposal was accepted, but it was an ordeal to convince my parents to let me do it. It was the new me that they were dealing with, however. I didn't wait for them to give me permission, I just started going. What could they do? Hit me? It seemed like they hit me no matter what I did.

Sometimes my father wouldn't let me in the house when I got home after 6 p.m. Once I had to stay out on the stairs all night. My mother said I was getting out of hand and my father agreed. "We are going to take her back to India as soon as she finishes this damn school," he said. This "American nonsense" was getting to me, they concluded.

Before, I would just stand there like a statue and take it. But not this time.

One day I came back from school and my father started hitting me with his belt. I was shocked—usually he would at least give a reason before he started beating me. I thought he had gone crazy. I just looked at him, too stunned to say anything. Then he stopped and said, "This is so that you can do your child abuse report better." Somehow, he had found out what my science project was about.

Later my mother grabbed me by the hair and started slapping me. "A report on child abuse," she chuckled. "How daring!" She slapped me again. "How daring!" she repeated. Slap! "Child abuse, hah!" Slap!

Suddenly I couldn't take it anymore. I pushed her away. Before, I would just stand there like a statue and take it when she hit me. But not this time. I left the room and locked myself in the bathroom. I cried a little, and thought about why they were so upset about my project. I knew other kids who were doing projects on dysfunctional families but their parents didn't get angry with them. It occurred to me for the first time that my parents knew that they were abusing me.

All along I had been thinking that they didn't know any better, that it was just the Indian custom to treat children this way. But they were perfectly aware of what they were doing. No wonder when my teachers spoke to my parents they always came away with the impression that my parents were just "overprotective." My parents had been treating me this way knowing it was wrong and making sure no one found out.

Suddenly I hated them. I had never felt as angry as I did that day. I used to think that it would be possible for us to have a reconciliation when I got older. But I no longer believe that there is any chance of that.

My parents still talk about taking me back to India to get all the "American crap" out of me. I have other plans, however. I'm going to stay here and study so I can help children like me as much as possible—not just in India, but all over the world. Because no one deserves to be treated the way I have been.

Zeena Bhattacharya was 16 when she wrote this story. She ultimately reported her parents' abuse and went into foster care. She has since graduated from Bard College.

Carla Chacón

Rookie Mistake

By Mohammed Hussain

Gym was about to begin. We 8th grade boys sat in rows brimming with the blues, greens, oranges, and reds of our gym clothes. Suddenly our loud banter turned into a silent murmur. Mr. O'Hara, the gym teacher, was speaking.

"Basketball tryouts will take place after school today in the gym," he announced.

I looked at the other boys and could see the excitement on their faces. Making the basketball team would be a dream come true: You'd get to play one of the greatest sports in America while having the honor of representing the school. Most importantly, you'd gain popularity, and with popularity came something else: girls. Few boys in that gym class would give up a chance to get popular with females.

All of this meant that the competition at tryouts would be fierce, but I loved competition and I wanted to be a part of the excitement. Even though I was rather short for my age, and couldn't play basketball well, by the end of the day, my mind was set. I would try out—even if it meant staying after school without my parents' permission.

Attending basketball tryouts would be better than going home. Home was the dungeon where my three little sisters outnumbered me. Any time I tried to watch my favorite TV shows, they changed the channel. Whenever I went on the computer, they'd ask me to show them episodes of the Simpsons. If I said no, they'd stay right there, giving me no chance to enjoy surfing the Internet alone.

And if I got annoyed and tried to hit one of my sisters, they'd all fight back: pulling my hair, throwing me on the ground, and punching me relentlessly. To top it all off, when my mother came to see what the commotion was, I was the one who'd get in trouble because I was older.

I also knew that at home, I'd have to deal with my mother's constant shouting to clean the dishes and not stay on the computer for long. My whole family is Bengali and we're the first of our lineage to live in America. Though my parents and grandmother came to this country to chase the American dream, they never chased Western ideals. They brought their rigid standards with them, and expected me to be devoted to my religion, my family, and my education. They expected me to spend less time on the computer than I wanted and generally obey their commands.

Although I was born in Bangladesh, I came to America at a young age. I feel more American than Bengali because I've grown up around this society and its more lax nature. But I've never felt completely free to enjoy this laxity because of my family. I used to imagine what it would like to be a typical American teenager, the youth who did whatever he wanted—going home late, always hanging out with friends, indulging in materialistic desires.

This idea was in my head when I decided to stay for basketball tryouts. Just for today, I thought, I want to be away from my mother's constant pestering. Just for today, I want independence.

I was fairly sure that staying after school for academic reasons would be acceptable to my parents, but staying for basketball would be out of the question. So I made up a lie to tell my mother: I would say I fell asleep on the bus and missed my stop. This lie would keep me from getting into trouble when I finally did get home. Reassured, I decided it was time to have fun playing basketball.

After school, I went into the gym for tryouts as I had planned. I left my jacket on the benches with my book bag and went to stand in line with the other boys.

For a moment, my eyes turned to the direction of the window. I saw the gloomy, gray sky. I could sense the approaching rain and the dark, ominous clouds; it gave me a queasy feeling and seemed to fore-shadow something bad. Guilt was creeping up on me; I knew I shouldn't be here, and I knew that lying to my mother about why I was late was immoral.

As those boys and I stood straight as soldiers, I felt powerful: I belonged here with them.

But as all those boys and I stood straight as soldiers, I felt powerful: I belonged here with them. I had the feeling you only get when you're with people who truly know you. In my home, I couldn't seem to find that feeling: my mom seemed to want to mold me into a perfect boy, and my younger sisters just thought about what they wanted. No one at home asked me about my day; no one bothered to try to understand my life.

My peers, however, shared the same goals. We all wanted to compete and have a good time. Each of us understood the others' feelings. Knowing this made me feel a mixture of power and confidence, as a person may feel before he sets out to accomplish a task that he knows he can fulfill.

Mr. O'Hara told us to do some general exercises—like running around the gym—and gave us tests that measured our basketball abilities, like shooting the ball while moving through an obstacle course. I wasn't any good, but I was having so much fun. Even if I missed shots or bumped into other students, it was great to be away from the responsibilities of home.

Even as I enjoyed myself, I wondered if I'd made a mistake by not notifying my mother. She had the right to know where I was. Still, I thought, she didn't have the right to boss me around all the time. It was really her fault, I rationalized, that I hadn't called. After all, if she didn't make me go through hell with all those chores, I wouldn't have to stay away to escape the madness.

Suddenly, late into the tryouts, I heard an announcement over the loudspeaker calling for one Mohammed Hussain to go down into the main office. I suddenly realized it was me they were calling. Once again, I had a queasy feeling. I had never before been called to the office. My footsteps made an eerie noise as I ran out of the gym and through the deserted halls. My hands were numb and my heart beat rapidly. Time seemed to have stopped.

I had a feeling I had been called because my parents were looking for me. They would find out I had acted selfishly and foolishly, which would mean punishment. I hoped that my mistake didn't result in fewer freedoms at home: no more video games or going on the Internet.

But when I got to the main office, video games slipped from my mind entirely. There was my mother in her black coat, her embroidered scarlet scarf on her head. My older sister, Farzana, stood next to her. I had expected anger, but what surprised me were the tears on my mother's face.

Her face had blotches of red, and those tears were carrying away what little mascara she wore. The way she looked at me— with a mixture of agony, relief, and joy—knocked some sense into me.

"Mom, Mom, what is wrong?" I asked her in Bengali. She hugged me tightly, as a blind man would hold a strand of light, but said nothing. Then Farzana looked at me in her usual, chastising way—like I was a two-year-old who was caught with his hand in the candy jar—and said: "I told her, 'He's probably at school doing something,' but she wouldn't listen. She thought you'd been kidnapped."

I couldn't believe what I was hearing. The outlandishness of what had gone through my mother's mind would have brought me to laughter in another situation, but not now. As I held my mother tightly, as though I was the parent and she was the baby, tears for the pain I had caused her began to flow freely from my eyes, too.

I felt like a miserable, worthless child—I had left my mother to suffer for the sake of my own selfish pleasure. Sharp knives of guilt cut through me. I didn't think about it at that moment, but maybe the reason I felt my mother's pain so much was that I had once felt the same worry about her, a few years before.

I had expected anger, but what surprised me were the tears on my mother's face.

During the blackout in August of 2003, my sisters, grandmother, and I were at home when, suddenly, the television turned off and all the power went out in our building. As the evening had worn on, my sisters and I had sat on our heater by the window, watching night fall. Darkness came, and my sense of worry grew: Many people's parents had come home, but mine had not. I was 10 years old and terrified at the thought of losing my parents; so terrified, in fact, that I began to believe they had died in an accident, unable to see in the pitch darkness of that night.

Now I had grown older and become so wrapped up in my own life that that it had never occurred to me that my parents might be worried in the same way about me. When I saw my mother the day of the tryouts, I realized how stupid I had been. I was thinking so much about me—my pains because of my mother's nagging—that I had forgotten what it's like to care about a loved one's safety.

I had also overlooked an important fact: my mother loves me. Her nagging is a sign of caring; because she wants me to become a better person, she makes me do the chores and limits my time on the computer.

"Mom, what is wrong?" I asked. She hugged me tightly, as a blind man would hold a strand of light.

Since that day, I've approached my family life differently. Whenever I get frustrated by constraints in my life or by my sisters' pestering, I remember that day and how lucky I am to have a family. I may crave certain freedoms that American teens have, but I've also seen how freedom can cause problems. I have a friend who has become addicted to drugs and sex; he is not even 18 years old yet. When I think about him, I'm grateful for that watchfulness I get at home. Maybe he could have avoided the wrong path if someone had watched him closely like my parents watch me.

I'm now a high school junior, and I've matured. I'm older, taller, and smarter. My voice has deepened and a few months ago, I shaved for the first time.

My relationship with my parents has developed, too. They are still protective of me; when I first came to work at Youth Communication last summer, they accompanied me to the office in Manhattan to make sure I found my way. Furthermore, I'm still expected to do chores and limit my computer time (although they've been less austere about these expectations).

But my parents realize I'm getting older, and they know age brings a greater degree of freedom. They let me hang out with friends now, because they trust that I will take care of myself.

Staying late after school is not a problem anymore, so long as I let my parents know ahead of time.

And as they've learned to respect my need for greater freedom, I've learned to appreciate my parents' excessive care. I know my parents' strictness has taught me good morals and proper behavior, which will make me more independent and responsible in the long run. Had my parents not been so strict, I might not have learned how to take good care of myself.

Mohammad was 15 when he wrote this story.

Lola Odunsi

American Schools Are Child's Play

By Anna Borshchevskaya

Since I came to this country three years ago, I can honestly say that I've hardly learned anything new—at least not in school.

From my experience, American schools just aren't strict enough. Teachers don't assign a lot of homework, or seem to care if you do it on time. I'm from Russia, where a teacher might tell a class to memorize a three-page poem for the next day. If a teacher did that here, the students would probably look at her like she was from another planet, or laugh in her face.

I remember my first day of school in Queens, New York. I was 12 years old and I was so scared that my blood was freezing like a popsicle in my veins. The surprise algebra tests they used to give us in Moscow still haunted me. I thought, "If I could barely pass them there, where everything was in my native language, how will I survive here?"

The first assignment they gave us that day was a grammar exercise, something like, "Fill in the blank: The dress __ ugly. Those people ___ old." I could do that when I was 8 and just starting to learn English back in Russia. I still remember the frightened look on the teacher's face when I handed in a finished paper just five minutes after she had passed it out.

The next day we had a math test where we had to solve problems like 2x-3 = 7, which was something I'd done two years before. I got 100 on that test. I wanted to laugh out loud the following day when my teacher told me how good I was at math. I wished my Russian math teacher could have heard this comment. The year before, I'd received a 'C' in her class. But here, I was a top math student. That's because at the end of my 8th grade year they were teaching me things that we had learned in 3rd grade in Moscow.

In this country, I got less homework in a week than I had every day in Russia for each of my classes. Because I was getting straight 'A's, people in my American class thought that all I did was study, but I rarely spent more than an hour a day on homework. I often did most of it at lunch, and when I came home, I didn't have to do anything.

"Don't you have any homework?" my mom kept asking me when I came home.

"I already finished it," I would say, but I don't think she believed me. It took her a while to get used to the idea that I didn't have to spend three to four hours a night on homework anymore.

Nevertheless, because of my grades, the teachers couldn't stop bragging about me. That only made me feel worse. It was like being proud of a 10-year-old because she can walk.

School in Russia was so strict that I always used to think about students and teachers as "us against them." But here, I honestly felt sorry for the teachers when they had to remind people to bring homework over and over again. No one even seemed to be listening. If you didn't bring your homework on time, you could bring it tomorrow. . . or the day after tomorrow, or the day after that. I got the impression that some teachers were just happy to get any homework from the students at all. It almost didn't matter if it was late or messy.

When things are this way, it teaches you not to take responsibility seriously. After all, why bother remembering anything if someone will always remind you, and if there are no consequences for not doing your work?

The teachers couldn't stop bragging about me. It was like being proud of a 10-year-old because she can walk.

I believe mistakes should carry consequences. And if a teacher asks you a question, you should have to answer it instead of just saying you don't want to—something that I've seen many students here do. When a teacher gives homework, you should be required to bring it on time. And if you don't meet that requirement you shouldn't be given the same grade as someone who did.

I always hated all the homework I had to do when I lived in Russia, but now I realize how much I learned because of it. Maybe they don't need to lower your grade for one misspelled word the way they do in my country, but at least the homework ought to be done. No matter how much we all hate rules (yes, even me), they teach discipline and respect, as well as self-respect.

The rules don't need to be extreme, but they need to exist. Without them, you never learn to finish what you start, to manage your time so that you get everything done, to be responsible, and to be punctual. And without learning these things, you're not likely to succeed.

Anna was 15 when she wrote this story. She graduated from college with a degree in political science and economics, and got a master's degree at Johns Hopkins.

Chapter 4:
Becoming American

Frantz David Bordes

BEFORE   AFTER

From a Whisper to a Scream

By Nana Ntsakey

At a friend's 6th birthday party in school, I was called up to the center of the class to say a few words. I went up with the glare of everybody's gaze directed straight into my face. I was only 7.

Questions started running through my mind about what I could and couldn't say. I had once seen a kid give a speech at a public gathering and it was as if an adult was speaking; everything was written for him by someone else. But I had no script. How could I say what I felt in a way that would not offend any of the many adults present?

I don't remember what I said, but it definitely wasn't what I'd wanted to say. I wished all the adults would disappear so I could have the freedom to talk. Their presence made me so nervous.

Growing up in the tropical city of Accra in Ghana, a country in West Africa, I had the understanding that adults were always right instilled in my blood. I was taught that what I as a child had to say was not important, and that expressing myself freely was a sign of disrespect. Adults didn't even like kids to talk with their hands; they interpreted this as kids being too bold. Many kids liked to use their hands for emphasis, but since they'd get punished if they gestured, they rarely did so in the presence of adults.

Everything a kid said was scrutinized to make sure it met the standards of a good upbringing. Adults taught children that saying little and being reserved in speech and manner was a sign of good character and respect for adults. Parents used to brag to other parents about how their kids were respectful, and saw outspoken or lively kids as failures. As one Ghanaian saying goes, "Every display of disrespect toward an adult is a year off one's lifespan."

At my school in Africa, a student could not look directly into a teacher's face when asking questions.

I have to admit that this reserved way of life did have some advantages. Because kids couldn't talk freely to adults, there was always an outward sense of discipline. It created an orderly society with clearly defined lines between the old and young.

But too often, that sense of order felt overbearing. At my school, a student could not look directly into a teacher's face when asking questions. Asking a question in class meant getting up from my seat and standing up while using words like "please" and "may I."

Students kept our heads and eyes low when talking to teachers to show that we were cultured. Class discussions rarely took place at school, because we couldn't explore our ideas for fear of offending the teacher and eventually being punished by what we called the "whip"—a strong verbal insult, or an actual beating with a cane.

I remember Jacob, a friend of mine in my 7th grade class, asking our math teacher why his response to a question was marked wrong.

"But Sir, this answer is right," Jacob said. "I tried a new method for solving it and clearly showed it in my work."

"Why didn't you use what I taught?" the teacher responded sharply. "You don't understand things as well as I do, so just follow my methods."

"Sir, it's just that maybe if we could use more methods and choose the easiest, everyone would be happy," Jacob responded. "Sir, you hardly give us a chance to ask. . ."

"I'm the teacher here. You insolent kid! Is this what your parents teach you at home?"

After that, the class was like a cemetery, quiet and motionless. Tension was so high that even breathing became hard. It was clear that the only permissible questions involved asking a teacher to go over a lesson. There were no "what ifs" in this classroom. I felt like what I had to say was of no importance.

At least it was a different ball game at home. I grew up living with my grandfather because my parents were always overseas in Europe and the United States. Grandpa didn't mind my curiosity. He said it was as inevitable as a baby crying. He saw it as part of the growth process and felt he had to provide a safe zone for me to express myself. At home, I could ask anything I wanted without looking over my shoulder to see who was watching or listening. I could ask Grandpa what was going on with the government, why people talked about chieftaincy disputes, and why the sky was up.

Writing was the other outlet through which I could express myself. I got into the habit of putting my emotions on paper in an attempt to imitate Grandpa, who always wrote. He encouraged me to put my ideas down where I could go back and read them. Once, I wrote about a perfect place where there were no walls between the old and young. I imagined a place where people allowed room for children's curiosities to run wild.

T hen, at 13, I moved to the United States. My mom, who was already here, wanted me to receive a better education. I was quite excited to cross over and experience a new culture, especially since I expected a difference in the way kids would relate to adults.

I was right. In America, I found a new definition of respect: To me, respect in America means sharing ideas and being able to open up to others without infringing upon their beliefs. Every time I see people arguing here it seems very constructive; each person, no matter their age, gets a chance to put forth his or her ideas. Back home, it was always a one-way street: Adults spoke and kids listened.

Even though I expected American kids would have more freedom, when I first saw how often questions flew at teachers here, I was taken aback. Could these youngsters really ask anything they wanted about a subject? Since then, I have seen a few kids go overboard in challenging the teacher. A student once asked a teacher where he went to college and got his teaching degree, which I read as, "Are you qualified to be a teacher?"

In America, each person, no matter their age, gets a chance to put forth his or her ideas.

But even in that instance, the teacher simply answered the questions without showing any signs of resentment or anger. I liked his composure. I grew to feel that the open type of environment you find in American classrooms makes learning easier, since students don't fear punishment for asking questions.

I gradually became more frank with adults, which felt uplifting. I would say hi to a teacher with a high five. In Ghana, this would have been seen as great disrespect. Once, one of my teachers made a joke about me, and I told him I didn't find it funny. If this were a Ghanaian setting, I'd have had to accept it.

As I got used to the idea of free speech, I felt like I'd been let loose with a credit card in a shopping mall; I just couldn't keep my mouth shut in a discussion, whether it was with my peers or with adults. I felt a new urge to express my views openly.

My parents noticed my upsurge in confidence and the freedom with which I expressed myself.

"Are you going to do your homework now or am I going to have to confiscate your console?" my mom once said when she came home and saw me playing a video game.

Almost reflexively, I replied, "I've done it already. It's on my desk if you want to check."

As I got used to free speech, I felt like I'd been let loose with a credit card in a shopping mall.

In Ghana, this would've been like slapping her in the face. But she just smiled and commented on how smoothly I was blending in.

I began to see every conversation as an opportunity to say what was in my heart. But there are times when I miss the old me. Sometimes I worry that I'm being insolent and rude, since I wasn't brought up like this. And my Ghanaian friends often say I've forgotten my morals and culture.

At family gatherings or when my parents have Ghanaian guests over, I'm expected to carry myself as if I'm back home. Whatever I say has to begin with "Please" and be said in a mellow voice, as if I was begging.

Some time ago, we had guests over and just as we were welcoming them with greetings and hugs, the phone rang. I answered; it was one of my classmates. Everyone was quiet and trying to listen in, so I put down the handset and picked up the phone in my room because I wanted privacy.

Immediately I could hear arguments about me going on in the living room. The guests thought I should have finished taking the call in front of them since, in Ghana, a child's privacy is as private as a public gathering. They felt I'd been given too much freedom and space.

This was a wake-up call. I realized there were times I still had to fit the traditional Ghanaian definition of a good kid to keep peace and shield my parents from criticism.

Nonetheless, being able to express myself openly most of the time is a great gift. My mind feels clearer and less burdened with worry. I find it easier to relate to people and understand different perspectives.

I'm learning to create a balance between what I grew up knowing and what I've come to learn. I feel like it's important for me to hold on to some parts of my native culture, no matter where I am in the world. I try hard to talk informally without going overboard in what I say by keeping my childhood memories fresh in my mind.

Nana was in high school when she wrote this story.

Odessa Straub

The Mom and Dad I Never Had

By Anonymous

My parents were teenagers in El Salvador when my mom got pregnant at 16. In our country, she and my dad didn't have many opportunities, so after she gave birth, they went to America, leaving me behind with my grandparents.

Growing up in El Salvador was depressing. In school, my classmates asked me where my parents were and I didn't know how to answer. One of my aunts told me that my parents abandoned me because they didn't want me. I used to go to the hills and wonder what my parents were like. I would ask myself why they left me. Why couldn't they take me with them?

When my parents got married, they sent my grandmother a wedding picture and she put it on the wall for me. I stood on a stool, got the picture, and threw it on the floor. My grandmother saw me and said, "You need to respect your parents!" Before she could slap my hand, I ran away and hid.

I was 8 years old when my parents brought me to the United States. Everything came as a shock to me. I couldn't believe how many cars were on the freeway in Los Angeles. My parents took me to McDonald's and when I saw the pancakes, I thought they were tortillas. On the radio I heard only English music; I wondered what they were saying.

Seeing my family was hard, too. It was very painful to meet my younger sister. I was angry because I felt my parents loved her more than me. I refused to call my parents "Mom" or "Dad."

I used to go to the hills and wonder what my parents were like and why they left me.

When my parents enrolled me in school, I cried because I didn't want to go. I was scared because I didn't know the language and I had never seen black people before. Since I couldn't read the street signs, I memorized the way so I could get back home.

Slowly I got used to living in L.A., but I didn't get along with my parents. Since they had left me in El Salvador, I felt they owed me. I thought that they should let me do whatever I wanted. In 8th grade I started smoking. I had to be home at a certain time, but I didn't like going home, so I used to tell my parents that I had detention or tutoring.

Sometimes I took classes that would be easy to pass so it wouldn't matter if I ditched. The days that I didn't go to school, I'd go with a friend to a restaurant and we would order something and never pick it up. Or we'd go to stores and try on clothes but never buy them.

In 9th grade, I started drinking. As long as I got straight A's, my dad wasn't concerned. But one day I was walking home and I saw a drunk man asking for money. I got scared that I would end up like that, so I decided to stop drinking.

At the end of 9th grade I met my boyfriend. We dated for a year without my parents knowing—I was not allowed to date. I felt my boyfriend really understood me. There was a big connection between us so I would do anything to see him. Even though I was supposed to go home right after school, he would take me out to eat. Or, if he had a soccer game, I would go see him play. One day when he walked me home, we got to talking and forgot about the time. My dad came home and found us talking. He was suspicious but I told him we were just friends.

One day my mom saw me at church with my boyfriend and she told my dad. They both wanted to know more about him, so I told them the truth. I decided to tell them about everything—the smoking, drinking, and sneaking around with my boyfriend. My dad got very quiet. When I finished, he had a very serious look. He said, "So this is all the bad stuff you've been doing." He was really angry and he blamed my boyfriend. My parents told me that my boyfriend couldn't call me anymore and that I was not allowed to see him at school or anywhere else.

After that we saw each other a lot less, only at school. Sometimes he would walk me halfway home. I was depressed. I used to ask my boyfriend why bad things happened to me if I didn't deserve them. My boyfriend would tell me jokes to cheer me up, but things that used to make me happy weren't working anymore. I started thinking about suicide. I told my boyfriend that I was tired of everything and if only I could end my life, I wouldn't have to deal with all my problems.

One Sunday night a friend called me, and my dad asked me if he was my boyfriend. I told him he wasn't but he didn't believe me. I didn't feel like arguing but my dad did, so we got into a fight. The last thing he told me was, "I can't wait for you to become 18 so you can be responsible for yourself and your actions. These next two years will seem like 20." That really hurt me. I thought that when a man and a woman decide to have a baby, it is forever and not until their child turns 18.

That night I went to bed crying and I decided to run away. Once I was sure that my parents were asleep, I left. I decided to go to my boyfriend's house because I don't get along with my uncles. The streets were foggy and lonely. It was really dark and dogs were barking. I was scared and I walked fast so that the police wouldn't see me. I was also afraid that my parents would notice me missing and come out looking for me.

At my boyfriend's house, I knocked on his window but he didn't answer, so I went to the front door. He came to the door, shocked to see me at that hour. He said, "What are you doing here at midnight? Are you OK? Did something happen?"

This year, I asked my dad to take me to the prom.

At first I couldn't answer him, I just cried. Then I told him that I had run away. I told him what happened, but neither of us knew what to do. We stayed up all night talking and the next day I went home because I didn't want the problem to get bigger.

When my parents got home from work that afternoon, they just looked at me. They didn't seem too happy to see me. The first thing my mom told me was, "Nobody will take care of you or support you." I just stayed quiet. My dad told me, "You are still under our responsibility—you can't do whatever you want! We take care of you for free—other people won't do that. If you're not going to be happy here, you can leave right now. Just say goodbye to your sister."

My little sister was crying when I hugged her and walked to the door. Just before I walked out, my mom grabbed me by the arm. She told me things don't work like that. She said I had to wait until I was 18.

I sat down on the living room couch. I was angry and sad at the same time. I didn't know if they really wanted me, or if they were afraid of getting in trouble with the police or a social worker or something.

My mom told me it was stupid to run away and put myself in danger. She said I only ran away so I could sleep with my boyfriend. That wasn't true, but I didn't contradict her because I knew it would just make things worse if I did.

My mom started laughing over the stupid decisions I had made. I was mad that she was laughing because if they had paid more attention to me, or asked me questions or listened to me, none of this would've happened.

Then my dad lectured me for a long time, telling me everything I could and couldn't do. I couldn't talk on the phone, listen to music, watch TV, or stay after school. I had to tell them everything I did. He wanted me to spend my spare time thinking about my bad decisions and to stop being a bad influence on my sister.

It was nothing new. He had gotten angry with me before. But he also said he was going to give me another chance. The next day my boyfriend went to my house to ask for permission to talk to me. My dad said he could come over, but only when my parents were there. When I asked my dad why he did that, he said, "We want you to trust us and we're going to trust you." I felt happy and hoped that things would get better, but I wondered if he would keep his word.

I noticed that my parents started keeping a closer eye on me. They'd ask me, "Are you doing bad things? Are you smoking? Are you drinking?" They were doing what they should have done all along. When my parents got home, I just pretended I was doing homework so we didn't have to talk. I felt weird. After everything that had happened, all of a sudden they wanted to be good parents.

Every night, I'd talk to my sister about them. We'd make fun of them and all the things they did. But I came right home after school and did my homework.

Slowly, as they saw me following the rules, they trusted me more. They let me stay after school to do projects, and they let my boyfriend come over. I could watch TV and use the phone again.

My mom came into my bedroom one night and got in bed with me. She hugged me and told me she was going to try to be more understanding. I cried because she had never done that before. She told me that all she wants is for me to graduate from high school, and not go through the things she went through at my age, like getting pregnant.

It's easier to talk to my dad now, too. Sometimes he lets me go out, if he feels I'll be safe and he knows where I will be. He lets me take my sister along if I want to, because he knows that I'll take care of her.

Recently my mom told me that you don't study to be a parent, you learn as you go along. Even though I'm almost 18, my mom is just starting to be the mom she wanted to be. Now that I'm a teenager, and I see classmates becoming mothers, I have more understanding for my parents' decision to leave me behind in El Salvador. I see how hard it is to be a parent at a young age.

And just like your parents have to learn, you have to learn. Finally I'm learning how to be a daughter. If I want to stay out of trouble, I have to tell them what I'm doing so they can give me advice. If something's bothering me, I can't assume my parents will know what's wrong.

My dad let me go to my boyfriend's prom. When I told my dad all about it, he said he'd never had the chance to go to something like that. So this year, I asked my dad to take me to the prom. He was so happy when I asked him. My friends think it's weird, but I told them I would like to share one of my senior activities with my dad.

It seems like sometimes something big has to happen for your parents to notice that you're there. Even though it was really hard, I'm glad that my parents and I are closer now. I'm going to graduate this year and make my parents proud. That's my way of paying them back for everything they have done for me.

The author was in high school when she wrote this story.

American at Heart— But Not on Paper

By Anonymous

The first time I went looking for work I was 15. I went to Modell's sports store because one of my friends had worked there and told me about his experience stocking shoeboxes in the back all by himself. He was like me and didn't like working with customers, so I figured the job would suit me perfectly, keeping me away from obnoxious people.

I grabbed an application from a box near the entrance of the store. As I rode the escalator to the second level, I filled out everything except the box for my Social Security number, and made my way to the registers.

I came face-to-face with the manager, who said, "Hello sir, welcome to Modell's. My name is Chris. How can I help you today?"

To increase the odds of him liking me, I decided to imitate his formal manner and extended my arm to shake his hand. I introduced myself and said, "I filled out this application in hopes of working with people who know how to do their jobs." I gave a wide grin and placed the application in his hand, right side up.

He must have been impressed with the way I handled myself, because on the spot he looked the application over. It didn't come as a surprise when he pointed out the missing Social Security number, even though I'd hoped he'd ignore it. I made an "Oh, that's what I forgot" gesture, then said, "I'll bring it in tomorrow since I can never remember numbers properly."

He smirked and told me, "For the future, try to memorize your Social, since it will haunt you all your life."

The truth was that I don't have a Social Security number, but it haunts me all the same. As an undocumented immigrant, I can't legally work in the United States. I exited the store feeling confident that I could have gotten the job, but also gloomy that I hadn't. I began to realize that my options for getting a job were severely limited.

Jobs that paid off the books didn't have a sign outside saying, "No Social? No problem!"

I arrived in the United States at age 5 with both my parents. People often believe I'm American-born, because I don't speak with an accent and my English is a bit better than my native language. Though I try to maintain my native culture, I feel "Americanized" because I also like learning from the diverse group of people all around me, the melting pot of ideas that makes America.

Despite this, I can't take part in the privileges most Americans enjoy, like driving a car or applying for a standard job, because my parents brought me here illegally when I was too young to have a say.

The Modell's manager ended up calling my house and leaving messages that the position was still available and they needed me ASAP. To get him off my back, I said I was failing school and couldn't be distracted by a job, but I'd say he figured out the truth.

I thought my situation was unfair, especially when I saw all my friends working and I wasn't allowed to take the same steps toward independence. No teenager wants to hassle his parents for money for the rest of his life; I needed a job. But jobs that paid off the books didn't have a sign outside saying, "No Social? No problem, we hire!"

I knew I could either dwell on the injustice and do nothing, or get creative. So that winter, I decided to risk catching a flu or fever shoveling snow from people's houses. I walked to Shore Road in Bay Ridge, a wealthy area in Brooklyn, New York where many residents are older and might need shoveling done.

Over two days, I made around $300 shoveling snow from driveways. In one home, the owners served me hot chocolate and a croissant; in another, I received a $100 check for helping a couple dig out their car.

I enjoyed the experience of manual work and meeting generous people, but I knew I couldn't do this all year. I needed to find a more stable source of income. One of my friends was in charge of handling flyers for jewelry stores, restaurants, and cell phone providers. We agreed that I would handle one or two routes for minimum wage, cash in hand.

The job was tedious. I had to stand on a street corner handing flyers to passersby. And I had to pick up any discarded flyers or I would get money deducted. After a while, I got tired of people throwing the flyers on the ground five feet away from me, so I quit.

Looking at my options, I began to understand that jobs with no set schedule or promised salary would leave me facing uncertainties all the time. But I wanted to buy a bike, so I had to do something.

The friends that I hung out with didn't have jobs but always had money. In my time of need, I realized they could give me a financial boost. I didn't need to ask what they did for money since I already knew. All I did was ask, "Can I help develop more customers?"

I started working with them in the underground economy. Money was abundant and in this job I didn't have to do any hard manual labor or distribute things alone. At first I just passed the word around the school about who sold what item and how great it was, like a walking advertisement.

Gradually I began ditching classes to hang out with these people. But I knew I could not sustain this lifestyle. Getting caught by the police would jeopardize my entire future—in my situation, the risk was not only jail, but possible deportation.

Besides this, I realized money wasn't the only reason I wanted a job. I also wanted to accomplish something with a larger meaning, not just help people consume things. Once I discovered that there were some things I didn't want to do for money, I stopped communicating with my old friends and decided to change my attitude.

I finally asked my father if I would be able to work with him. I had been reluctant to do this because I had bad childhood memories of him taking me to work with him. I was stubborn and wouldn't listen to him, and I didn't like it when he would yell at me for making a mistake.

Yet as a handyman he's made many good connections, since he does a professional job on construction, electrical, and plumbing projects. Working with him again as a teenager reminded me I can always earn an honest living doing what he does.

I also started working in a video game store, because I wanted the chance to do something different. Of course, it was off the books. But then the store underwent a change in management, and the new bosses wanted all employees to bring in documentation and appear on the store's payroll. That was the end of that job.

More recently, I began advertising my services as a repairman for musical instruments. The ads have brought me a few jobs so far. I'm hoping to develop my craftsman skills and one day turn my hobby into a steady income.

I've gotten so used to the obstacles I face that they're not a big deal anymore. I know that if I want a job, I have to look harder than most people. I see this as less of a headache than you might expect, because I believe my efforts make me stronger. I try to use frustrating experiences to increase my determination, instead of believing that because of my parents' decisions I'm condemned.

As far as a long-term plan for supporting myself, I haven't had much time to think about it, since I've been busy trying to finish high school. Besides, I've lived as an American in many ways for most of my life, so sometimes immigration problems don't seem quite real.

My dream is to become a teacher, because I want to help develop good citizens as well as good students. Unfortunately, I know it will be hard to pursue that kind of meaningful employment without documentation. It would be disappointing to have to relinquish my goals just because I need to make money to support myself. I don't want to take any job that comes my way just to get by.

I'm hoping to develop my craftsman skills and turn my hobby into a steady income.

My alternatives, though, are to move back to a country that is practically foreign to me, or live life under a fake identity and face more problems. So I'll do what I have to do to survive, while looking for ways to make my life fulfilling.

I will attend community college, continue to learn from people I meet, and volunteer around my neighborhood. My desire is to contribute to society and help my community prosper, and in this sense I don't need to be a citizen to be a good American or find satisfaction in what I do.

The author was 19 when he wrote this story. He graduated from high school in 2008.

Anna Jakimiuk-Chu

Sharing the American Dream

By Anna Jakimiuk-Chu

One Sunday in June, the Statue of Liberty stood under the platform of the #7 subway train in Queens, asking anyone who would listen, "Can you hear me? Can you hear me?"

A crowd of immigrants gathered around her responded, "Yes, yes!"

Then the Statue of Liberty asked, "What do you want?" and in one loud and clear voice, they said, "We want equal opportunity and equal access to college!"

The Statue of Liberty was played by 17-year-old Santiago. Like me, he is an immigrant and was an intern at Global Kids, an organization that teaches teens about activism.

As the Statue of Liberty, Santiago's face was serious as he recited his lines. Even though we rehearsed those very lines with him dozens of times, when our performance was finally presented, the words were both powerful and inspiring.

I think I felt so inspired because I believe that this is what America is all about: a place where everyone deserves a chance to follow their dreams, and in turn to make America a better place for everyone else who has a dream.

Our Statue of Liberty street theater was part of Global Kids' effort to create awareness of the DREAM Act. The DREAM Act (which stands for Development, Relief and Education for Alien Minors) is a bill that Congress is considering making into a law. It would allow some immigrant youth who have grown up in the United States but don't have legal immigrant status to become legal residents and, eventually, citizens.

DREAM Act supporters argue that undocumented kids shouldn't be penalized for their parents' decisions.

Various versions of the DREAM Act have been proposed in both the House and the Senate since 2001, but so far none of these measures have received enough votes to be passed. The most recent version was introduced to both houses in March 2009.

Under the DREAM Act, there are certain requirements that young immigrants would have to meet. They must have come to the U.S. before their 16th birthday and lived here for at least five years consecutively. They'll need to be between 12 and 35 by the time it's enacted to be covered by the act. They'll also have to have have a high school diploma or GED, and demonstrate good moral character; they can't have committed any crimes or be considered a "security risk" by the U.S. government.

If it's passed, the DREAM Act would affect up to 65,000 undocumented teens who graduate from U.S. high schools every year. Not only would it give many of these teens a path to citizenship, it would make college more affordable for them. Since 2002, U.S. rules have required undocumented immigrants to be charged out-of-state tuition for public colleges and universities, even if they have lived in the state and gone to public school since kindergarten.

DREAM Act opponents say that's just too bad. Senator Jon Kyl, a Republican from Arizona, has argued that immigrants without the proper documents—no matter how old they were when they came here—are still in this country illegally.

According to Kyl and others against the DREAM Act, those kids have already benefited from a free public education and should not get any privileges, like in-state tuition, because they are breaking immigration law. Opponents also worry that the DREAM Act would encourage more parents to bring their children here illegally.

But DREAM Act supporters argue that these undocumented kids weren't old enough to choose to come here, so they shouldn't be penalized for their parents' decisions. These students have worked hard, and many are successful in their schools or communities. If they get a college education, they could contribute even more to this country.

To escape violence, my friend Elisa (not her real name) came to the U.S. from Colombia with her father, mother, and an older brother. Guerrilla groups in Colombia that had been fighting the government for more than 40 years had gotten involved with the dangerous drug trade and were killing innocent people. "They arrived in little towns near my city causing terror and making people leave," she said.

Elisa came to New York on a tourist visa; she has relatives here from her father's side. Her family didn't apply for legal residency before they came, so when her tourist visa expired, Elisa was here illegally.

Despite her illegal status, Elisa is a respectable member of society. Now a senior in high school, she's been involved in many leadership activities, including student government. When she came to America five years ago, she didn't know a word of English, but now she gets high grades even in the college classes she takes through her high school.

Even though Elisa is a great student, all her hard work might be for nothing. Because of her undocumented status, Elisa won't be able to get financial aid, so she and her family will have to pay the full cost of attending college. If they can't afford it, she won't be able to go. And it's hard for illegal immigrants to find decent jobs, even with a college education.

I'm lucky that I'm not in Elisa's shoes. When I came here from Poland two and a half years ago, I was fortunate enough to become a citizen quickly because my mother, who'd moved to the U.S. when I was little, was already a citizen.

But to help people like Elisa, who want to continue their education and achieve their American dream, I took part in the Global Kids street theater in Queens.

My role that day was to collect signatures to send to Congress, showing people's support of the DREAM Act. Usually it makes me annoyed when people stop me on the street and try to get me to sign something. I have to say that it wasn't easy to be on the other side.

Many people didn't want to be bothered by teenagers who were making a lot of noise, and some Americans reacted disrespectfully to the question we asked: "Would you like to help undocumented immigrants by signing our petition?" I found out that they are not happy about the number of immigrants here. One even said something like, "You should go back to the country where you came from!"

However, most people were friendly and understanding. They smiled at us and wished us good luck in our mission. We collected about 500 signatures; each one was worth a lot to us. It felt like we were making an incredible difference.

Anna was 19 when she wrote this story.

YC Art Dept.

Why Not an Immigrant President?

By Angelica Molero

I was born in Peru but have lived in New York City since I was 6. It has become my home. Even though I don't plan to run for president, it would be nice to have that option. But the Constitution states that only native-born citizens of the U.S. are eligible to be president.

Some lawmakers have proposed changing this. In 2003 Senator Orrin G. Hatch, a Republican from Utah, proposed a constitutional amendment to allow immigrants who have been citizens of the U.S. for at least 20 years to run for president.

"Ours is a nation of immigrants," Hatch declared to the Senate upon presenting his amendment, known as the Equal Opportunity to Govern Amendment.

Hatch is a friend of Arnold Schwarzenegger, a former actor

who moved to the United States from Austria in 1968 and later became governor of California. Not surprisingly, Schwarzenegger supports the amendment. In 2004 he said on the TV show *Meet the Press* that "times have changed...there are so many people here in this country now from overseas who are immigrants who are doing a terrific job."

Immigrants who want to become naturalized citizens must endure a slow and difficult process. My mother is in the middle of applying for citizenship. She has long and tedious forms to fill out, endless fees to pay, and an exam on the history of the nation to pass before she can call herself a U.S. citizen. When immigrant citizens have so clearly demonstrated their loyalty and love for America, why should they be excluded from the presidency of the country?

There shouldn't be a difference between the treatment of natural-born and naturalized citizens.

Legal scholar Noah Feldman told *The New York Times* in 2003 that keeping immigrants out of the White House is "creating, in a way, a kind of second-class citizenship." I agree. When you become a citizen, that's it—you're a citizen. There shouldn't be a difference between the treatment of natural-born and naturalized citizens.

But the Constitution can't be changed without a great deal of public support. In order for a constitutional amendment to be passed, two-thirds of both the House of Representatives and the Senate must vote in favor of it. Then the amendment has to be approved by three-quarters of the nation's 50 state legislatures.

Experts agree that any immigrants-for-president amendment will be especially challenging to pass, because the U.S. has a tradition of distrusting immigrants' political loyalties. The framers of the Constitution included the "natural born" clause to begin with because they were afraid that an immigrant president would be more loyal to his home country than to the U.S. During World War II, the government made Japanese residents of the U.S. leave their homes and live in internment camps. More recently, in the wake of September 11th, the Justice Department has held some immigrants for months without charging them with a crime.

I hope that the public will overcome this kind of suspicion of immigrants. Someone who has gone through the rigors of becoming a citizen and has lived here for 20 or more years deserves the right to run for president, wherever they happen to have been born.

Angelica was 17 when she wrote this story.
She later attended Bard College.

Micah Zurer

When I Learned English
I Found My Voice

By Sandra Paucar

When I came to the United States from Ecuador four years ago, I had to adjust to many changes. The biggest of all was adjusting to the language. In my country, I was a good student. But in school here, I felt like I was set apart from the "normal" kids who spoke English. It was difficult to accept not being able to communicate with anyone I wanted and knowing I couldn't make English-speaking friends.

When I first arrived, I expected it would be easy to learn English. I thought it would be similar to Spanish and that you would write things the way they sounded. But after I started ESL classes, I began to see that it was going to be hard.

When I registered for 7th grade at a middle school in Brooklyn, I was placed in a bilingual class with other Spanish-speaking

students. My mother and I both believed that bilingual education was the best choice for students like me who didn't know
any English. We thought that by taking all my subject classes in
Spanish and taking English as a Second Language (ESL) classes
at the same time, I wouldn't fall behind.

On my second day of school here, we had a spelling test in
ESL. I didn't know about it, so I didn't study. When the teacher
gave the test, I was like, "What is he saying?"

"One, two, three..." the teacher dictated.

I couldn't understand him. I wrote every word the way it
sounded to me: "uan, tu, tri."

You can imagine how I did. When the teacher gave me my
paper back, I saw a big zero. I felt like a loser, a dumb good-for-
nothing, because in my country I was a girl with good grades. It
made me feel like I was pressed to the wall and worth less than
people who knew English.

But besides ESL class once a day and gym once a week, almost
all my classes were taught in Spanish. Having only two classes
in English was good for a while because I could concentrate
on my regular work like math,
social studies, and science. By
the middle of the school year,
though, I could see I wasn't
learning English fast enough.
After a year in the United States
and half a year in school, I could only understand a little.

Being unable to understand even simple conversations made me feel isolated.

For instance, I could go to a ticket window to buy train tickets
and make myself understood, but I might not understand if the
ticket seller asked me something. Being unable to understand
even simple conversations made me feel isolated. At school,
I used to watch the English-speaking students at lunch, and I
envied their ability to speak to whomever they wanted. It became
my goal to be able to communicate like them.

This was easier said than done, because I didn't have any
friends who could speak English. I couldn't even eat with English

speakers during lunch: The three bilingual classes ate in the cafeteria at the same time as the regular classes, but all the classes sat separately.

Although it was not the school's intention to segregate students, I still felt segregated. It didn't help that some English-speaking students looked at the bilingual students as inferior. Some would push us when they saw us in the halls; once, an English-speaking student swore at me.

I wanted to defend myself, but since I couldn't speak English, I thought I'd better stay quiet.

*E*ven when the English speakers weren't trying to make us feel inferior, I felt that way. As time went on, I wanted to know more teachers, to be involved in extracurricular activities, and to have people outside the bilingual program get to know me. But since I couldn't communicate, I felt alone and left out. I signed up for a video class in English, but I just sat there because the teacher didn't push me to get involved, and I was too shy to ask questions.

In 8th grade, I felt less and less shy about speaking English. I made my parents buy an instructional book for me on learning the language faster.

It helped me with things like pronouns, the days of the week, the months of the year, and numbers. I was learning some of these things at school, but with the book I was able to move faster.

I also started to go to the library to take out easy English books like *The Magic School Bus*. I started listening to English-language radio stations and watching sitcoms in English. At first I would just watch the actors' gestures and actions, but little by little I began to understand what they were saying.

I did everything I could to learn more. Whenever I didn't know the meaning of words I heard at school, I would stay after class and ask the teacher the meaning, pronunciation and spelling. I took a summer class in English, because when I stayed at home or hung out with my friends, nobody knew English and I couldn't practice.

Still, it wasn't until I went to high school that I became fluent. My school is an alternative high school with students from many different countries. Most of the students come to the school hardly speaking any English, but since all their classes are taught in English, they are forced to learn quickly.

At first, I would sit in class and not understand much. When I didn't understand, I

Whenever I didn't know the meaning of words I heard at school, I would stay after class and ask the teacher.

would ask somebody next to me who spoke Spanish. I would use very simple words in my writing assignments. Little by little, I began understanding more English. After only a year at this school, I was able to understand and speak English well.

Being in a school where all the students are learning the language makes me feel like I can join activities without being self-conscious. I can get to know English-speaking teachers, and if I have questions, I don't feel too shy to ask. I can finally read books at my grade level, like Richard Wright's novel *Native Son*, which I just finished. I listen to American music and even sing along.

Besides learning the language, I've learned another important lesson. My example can show others that if you want to do something and try hard, you can do it. I feel very proud of that.

Sandra was 16 when she wrote this story. She later graduated from City College of New York with a degree in psychology.

Clara Soh

Putting My Foot Down in a Place I Call Home

By Francis Madi

One day when I was 7, I went into my bedroom and saw my mother packing my stuff. I didn't ask why. Instead I asked, "Where are we going now?"

"We're moving to Cantaura," she said, referring to a small town in Venezuela, two hours away from the town of Puerto La Cruz, where we lived at the time.

I saw her sadness and I didn't want to show her I was disappointed too. So I said, "OK, how can I help?"

"I want you to help your brother pack up his toys," she answered.

"Yes, Mami." I walked away, but deep inside I wanted to run and burst out in tears.

I didn't want to leave Puerto La Cruz, with its beautiful

beaches and our beautiful house with my own room and a huge garden. After school, Mami would take my younger brother and me to the beach and we'd play in the sand after a refreshing battle against the waves. Living in Puerto La Cruz was the happiest time in my whole life.

But we never stayed in any one house, school, or city for long. When we lived in Venezuela, where I was born, my mother moved us to four different cities and five different houses. We switched schools eight times, sometimes because we'd moved and other times because she just decided to send us to a different school.

The way Mami sees it, she's always tried to reach for the stars, following her dreams to the next house, city, or country. But that's not the way I see it, because we've moved for other reasons besides her dreams. Sometimes she wanted to leave our house or town because she was fighting with the neighbors or the landlord. Other times we'd leave because she was having problems with her family or her job.

The way Mami sees it, she's always reached for the stars, following her dreams to the next house, city, or country.

My younger brother Alejandro and I never complained about moving, because Mami was the only person who supported us. We've seen her fight against everything, even her own family's opinions about her habits. We didn't want to add to the conflict in her life, so we accepted her decisions without questioning them.

But it's always been tough for me to move to a new place and adapt to new people and customs. I've often felt annoyed and frustrated at my mother's decisions because it seemed like she hadn't considered my feelings. Every time I settled into a new place and made friends at school, I had to move again. It made me feel frustrated and sad.

I was 4 the first time we moved, when my mother was leaving my father. We left Caracas, the capital of Venezuela, to move to Puerto La Cruz. When we moved to Cantaura, I started 2nd grade at a school 30 minutes away from home. A year later, we went back to Caracas because Mami had landed a good-paying job as a publicist.

My brother and I started 3rd grade at a private school in Caracas, which we hated because we didn't have any friends. That year, I was feeling hopeless about moving so much, so I decided not to make friends anymore. I wanted to protect myself from the pain of losing people when we moved again.

In 4th grade, Mami transferred us to another private school in Caracas so we'd be closer to home. For 5th grade, she chose to send us to a teacher's house in Caracas for private tutoring so we'd get better attention. But in the middle of the year, she decided my brother and I should be playing with other kids, so she put us back into a regular school.

I'd rarely had the chance to spend more than a year at one school.

For 6th grade, she sent me to an all-girls school. I felt optimistic for the first time in a long time, because she promised me I'd finish high school there. I wish she hadn't made a promise she couldn't keep.

I couldn't have predicted that our biggest move would be inspired by Venezuela's presidential election. In 1999, my mother was working as a publicist, helping companies publish their ads in newspapers. But after Venezuelan President Hugo Chavez was elected that year and started making changes to the government, many newspapers criticized his decisions.

Mami's clients stopped publishing their ads for fear of appearing to support the newspapers' opinions of the government. Each month her pay dropped further. Toward the end of 2002, when I was 13, Mami started talking to an old Venezuelan friend, Karina, who was living in New York. "Please, Carmen, come to New York," Karina said. "You know the situation there isn't going to change."

As soon as I heard Karina's idea, I figured my mother would

start planning to move to New York. She wouldn't just look at the stars—she'd try to reach them and drag us with her.

The night she came into my bedroom in Caracas and closed the door, my brother and I knew she was going to say something serious because she turned off the TV. She sat next to us and in a low voice said, "Kids, we're moving to New York City."

I'd known it was coming but I was still surprised. I'd imagined moving to another country but never New York, which I thought of as overcrowded and polluted. I knew it would be a huge change in culture and language.

But I didn't have much of a choice. I might have been able to stay in Venezuela with my father, but I didn't really know him. He called us twice a week and visited once a month, and that was it. I thought I wouldn't feel comfortable living with him.

I never cried during my last days in Venezuela, probably because I knew moving was part of my life. I'd given up thinking Mami would ever change. But I do remember going to say goodbye to friends and staff at school, and feeling a lump rise in my throat.

I felt so sad and frustrated because that was the first school I'd ever stayed at for more than two years. I liked talking with my classmates and teachers about a funny incident or subject from the year before. It was a novelty because I'd rarely had the chance to spend more than a year at one school.

I wanted to close myself in a cage forever and not have to feel the pain of leaving everyone and everything I knew. I was terribly upset with my mother but I still didn't have the courage to tell her I didn't want to move.

We moved to New York in the winter. I entered a middle school in Queens, where I was supposed to learn the basics of English (I didn't) and finish 8th grade (I did). The first person I met at that school was Maria from Colombia, a girl who made a big difference in my life. She made me feel welcome in that little school, in this language, and in this country. She's still my best friend, although we go to different schools, and I think our friendship will last forever.

For 9th grade, I went to a high school for recent immigrants in Queens. There I met more people like me, including Fio-Pio and Brunito from Peru, and Gaby from Chile. They also felt lost in this new culture, but most of all they hated moving—just like me.

After three years at Newcomers HS, I realized something inside me was starting to disappear, and it felt good. What was vanishing was that locked cage that had closed me off from the world, from my feelings, from other people. I wasn't going through life alone anymore. Finally, I could proudly say that my school was my second home, and that made me so happy.

I was sick of the word "moving." And I wanted to stand up for myself for once.

But Mami did not change. In our first years living in the U.S., we moved twice within Queens, for the usual reasons: My mother had fights with friends and neighbors and said she couldn't stand seeing them anymore. I was OK with these moves because I could still go to Newcomers HS. But at the end of 11th grade, my nightmare returned.

I remember it was a Thursday. Mami came to us and repeated that sentence she'd said so many times before: "Kids, we're moving." We knew without her saying anything else where we were going—Long Island. She'd gotten a new job there a few months before, and she was always getting home late.

I was finally fed up. For the first time in my life, I decided to fight for what I wanted. I was happy at Newcomers HS and I had good teachers and friends. I wanted to stay there for my senior year.

Even though I knew Mami's decision was final, I still asked her, "Couldn't we just move to another place in Queens?"

"Francis, you know how hard it is for me to go every day from Queens to my job in Long Island," she said. "You guys never appreciate the sacrifices I make."

Instead of accepting what she said, for the first time I asked myself, "Did I ever ask for those sacrifices? Am I that selfish? What about my sacrifices?"

I'd never complained about moving before—but did she ever listen to my needs? Did she ever stop to ask if I wanted to move from Puerto La Cruz or Caracas?

It was time for me to say what I was feeling. I was tired of changing schools and losing friends. I was sick of the word "moving." And I wanted to stand up for myself for once.

"Well, I'm staying at Newcomers no matter what," I said. "I don't care how far it is or how long it's going to take me. I'm not changing schools."

To my surprise, she supported my decision. "OK, you can still go," she said. But she warned me, "You're the one who is going to have to deal with your grades."

I knew my last year would be hard. It only took me 15 minutes to get to school when I lived in Queens, and from Long Island it would take me over an hour. But it was worth it to me.

Since I made my decision, my relationship with Mami has changed. She treats me more like a grown-up. Sometimes we listen to each other, like best friends do. Maybe it's wishful thinking, but I think I see in her eyes that she wants to see me graduate from Newcomers HS.

And while I appreciate everything Mami's done for us, I know I may have to stand up again in the future and do what's best for me, even if it means going against her will.

Recently, after only two months in our new apartment, Mami told me that she was upset with our landlord for not doing some promised repairs. She decided to move again. This time, at least, we moved closer to my school, which made things easier for me. It made me think that she's taking me seriously.

I like adventures, but enough is enough. I don't want to reach for the stars. I'd rather admire them glowing in the sky. I want to stay in one place and make friends I can keep.

I'm also relieved and somehow feel an inner peace because I've learned to stand up for myself. I'm becoming independent, and I'm looking forward to living on my own so I get to decide when to move or stay put.

And if I have a family sometime in the future, I can promise my future children that we'll stay in one place. I want them to be able to look back and say, "This is the house and the school where I grew up!"

Francis was 17 when she wrote this story.
She went on to attend college.

Teens:
How to Get More Out of This Book

Self-help: The teens who wrote the stories in this book did so because they hope that telling their stories will help readers who are facing similar challenges. They want you to know that you are not alone, and that taking specific steps can help you manage or overcome very difficult situations. They've done their best to be clear about the actions that worked for them so you can see if they'll work for you.

Writing: You can also use the book to improve your writing skills. Each teen in this book wrote 5-10 drafts of his or her story before it was published. If you read the stories closely you'll see that the teens work to include a beginning, a middle, and an end, and good scenes, description, dialogue, and anecdotes (little stories). To improve your writing, take a look at how these writers construct their stories. Try some of their techniques in your own writing.

Resources on the Web

We will occasionally post Think About It questions on our website, www.youthcomm.org, to accompany stories in this and other Youth Communication books. We try out the questions with teens and post the ones they like best. Many teens report that writing answers to those questions in a journal is very helpful.

How to Use This Book in Staff Training

Staff say that reading these stories gives them greater insight into what teens are thinking and feeling, and new strategies for working with them. You can help the staff you work with by using these stories as case studies.

Select one story to read in the group, and ask staff to identify and discuss the main issue facing the teen. There may be disagreement about this, based on the background and experience of staff. That is fine. One point of the exercise is that teens have complex lives and needs. Adults can probably be more effective if they don't focus too narrowly and can see several dimensions of their clients.

Ask staff: What issues or feelings does the story provoke in them? What kind of help do they think the teen wants? What interventions are likely to be most promising? Least effective? Why? How would you build trust with the teen writer? How have other adults failed the teen, and how might that affect his or her willingness to accept help? What other resources would be helpful to this teen, such as peer support, a mentor, counseling, family therapy, etc.

Resources on the Web

From time to time we will post Think About It questions on our website, www.youthcomm.org, to accompany stories in this and other Youth Communication books. We try out the questions with teens and post the ones that they find most effective. We'll also post lesson for some of the stories. Adults can use the questions and lessons in workshops.

Discussion Guide

Teachers and Staff:
How to Use This Book in Groups

When working with teens individually or in groups, you can use these stories to help young people face difficult issues in a way that feels safe to them. That's because talking about the issues in the stories usually feels safer to teens than talking about those same issues in their own lives. Addressing issues through the stories allows for some personal distance; they hit close to home, but not too close. Talking about them opens up a safe place for reflection. As teens gain confidence talking about the issues in the stories, they usually become more comfortable talking about those issues in their own lives.

Below are general questions to guide your discussion. In most cases you can read a story and conduct a discussion in one 45-minute session. Teens are usually happy to read the stories aloud, with each teen reading a paragraph or two. (Allow teens to pass if they don't want to read.) It takes 10-15 minutes to read a story straight through. However, it is often more effective to let workshop participants make comments and discuss the story as you go along. The workshop leader may even want to annotate her copy of the story beforehand with key questions.

If teens read the story ahead of time or silently, it's good to break the ice with a few questions that get everyone on the same page: Who is the main character? How old is she? What happened to her? How did she respond? Another good starting question is: "What stood out for you in the story?" Go around the room and let each person briefly mention one thing.

Then move on to open-ended questions, which encourage participants to think more deeply about what the writers were feeling, the choices they faced, and they actions they took. There are no right or wrong answers to the open-ended questions.

Open-ended questions encourage participants to think about how the themes, emotions, and choices in the stories relate to their own lives. Here are some examples of open-ended questions that we have found to be effective. You can use variations of these questions with almost any story in this book.

—What main problem or challenge did the writer face?

—What choices did the teen have in trying to deal with the problem?

—Which way of dealing with the problem was most effective for the teen? Why?

—What strengths, skills, or resources did the teen use to address the challenge?

—If you were in the writer's shoes, what would you have done?

—What could adults have done better to help this young person?

—What have you learned by reading this story that you didn't know before?

—What, if anything, will you do differently after reading this story?

—What surprised you in this story?

—Do you have a different view of this issue, or see a different way of dealing with it, after reading this story? Why or why not?

Credits

The stories in this book originally appeared in the following
Youth Communication publications:

"A New World Full of Strangers," by Edwidge Danticat, *New Youth Connections*, September/October 1987; "More Than Lions and Poverty," by Aissata Kebe, *New Youth Connections*, January/February 2006; "Tongue-Tied," by Amy Huang, *New Youth Connections*, September/October 2002; "Becoming A Different Person," by Daniel Verzhbo, *Represent*, January/February 2008; "Rich Country, Hard Life," by Raquel Fernandes, *New Youth Connections*, April 1995; "Moonlit Memories," by Chun Lar Tom, *New Youth Connections*, November 2002; "No Place to Call Home," by Mohammad Ali, *New Youth Connections*, April 2000; "Saying Goodbye," by Agelta Arqimandriti, *New Youth Connections*, January/February 2000; "A Goat Named Manush," by David Etienne, *New Youth Connections*, April 2008; "Other Ways to Be Rich," by Leneli Liggayu, *New Youth Connections*, September 2006; "My Family Across the Ocean," by Anonymous, *New Youth Connections*, November 2008; "My Chinese Family—Not Like TV," by Yuh-Yng Lee, *New Youth Connections*, November 1991; "Can I Have Both?" by Fanny Brito, *New Youth Connections*, September/October 2003; "Not My Father's Daughter," by Sarvenaz Ezzati, *New Youth Connections*, September 1993; "University of Kitchen?" by Orubba Almansouri, *New Youth Connections*, March 2009; "Too American for My Boyfriend," by Sue Chong, *New Youth Connections*, November 1991; "Home Is Where the Hurt Is," by Zeena Bhattacharya, *New Youth Connections*, September/October 1993; "Rookie Mistake," by Mohammed Hussain, *New Youth Connections*, December/January 2009-2010; "American Schools Are Child's Play," by Anna Borshchevskaya, *New Youth Connections*, December 1996; "From a Whisper to a Scream," by Nana Nsakey, *New Youth Connections*, March 2003; "American at Heart—But Not on Paper," by Anonymous, *New Youth Connections*, May/June 2008; "Sharing the American DREAM," by Anna Jakimiuk-Chu, *New Youth Connections*, January/February 2004; "Why Not an Immigrant President?" by Angelica Molero, *New Youth Connections*, September/October 2004; "When I Learned English I Found My Voice," by Sandra Paucar, *New Youth Connections*, May/June 1998; "Putting My Foot Down in a Place I Call Home," by Francis Madi, *New Youth Connections*, September/October 2006.

About
Youth Communication

Youth Communication, founded in 1980, is a nonprofit youth development program located in New York City whose mission is to teach writing, journalism, and leadership skills. The teenagers we train become writers for our websites and books and for two print magazines: *New Youth Connections*, a general-interest youth magazine, and *Represent*, a magazine by and for young people in foster care.

Each year, up to 100 young people participate in Youth Communication's school-year and summer journalism workshops, where they work under the direction of full-time professional editors. Most are African-American, Latino, or Asian, and many are recent immigrants. The opportunity to reach their peers with accurate portrayals of their lives and important self-help information motivates the young writers to create powerful stories.

Our goal is to run a strong youth development program in which teens produce high quality stories that inform and inspire their peers. Doing so requires us to be sensitive to the complicated lives and emotions of the teen participants while also providing an intellectually rigorous experience. We achieve that goal in the writing/teaching/editing relationship, which is the core of our program.

Our teaching and editorial process begins with discussions

between adult editors and the teen staff. In those meetings, the teens and the editors work together to identify the most important issues in the teens' lives and to figure out how those issues can be turned into stories that will resonate with teen readers.

Once story topics are chosen, students begin the process of crafting their stories. For a personal story, that means revisiting events in one's past to understand their significance for the future. For a commentary, it means developing a logical and persuasive point of view. For a reported story, it means gathering information through research and interviews. Students look inward and outward as they try to make sense of their experiences and the world around them and find the points of intersection between personal and social concerns. That process can take a few weeks or a few months. Stories frequently go through ten or more drafts as students work under the guidance of their editors, the way any professional writer does.

Many of the students who walk through our doors have uneven skills, as a result of poor education, living under extremely stressful conditions, or coming from homes where English is a second language. Yet, to complete their stories, students must successfully perform a wide range of activities, including writing and rewriting, reading, discussion, reflection, research, interviewing, and typing. They must work as members of a team and they must accept individual responsibility. They learn to provide constructive criticism, and to accept it. They engage in explorations of truthfulness, fairness, and accuracy. They meet deadlines. They must develop the audacity to believe that they have something important to say and the humility to recognize that saying it well is not a process of instant gratification. Rather, it usually requires a long, hard struggle through many discussions and much rewriting.

It would be impossible to teach these skills and dispositions as separate, disconnected topics, like grammar, ethics, or assertiveness. However, we find that students make rapid progress when they are learning skills in the context of an inquiry that is personally significant to them and that will benefit their peers.

When teens publish their stories—in *New Youth Connections* and *Represent*, on the web, and in other publications—they reach tens of thousands of teen and adult readers. Teachers, counselors, social workers, and other adults circulate the stories to young people in their classes and out-of-school youth programs. Adults tell us that teens in their programs—including many who are ordinarily resistant to reading—clamor for the stories. Teen readers report that the stories give them information they can't get anywhere else, and inspire them to reflect on their lives and open lines of communication with adults.

Writers usually participate in our program for one semester, though some stay much longer. Years later, many of them report that working here was a turning point in their lives—that it helped them acquire the confidence and skills that they needed for success in college and careers. Scores of our graduates have overcome tremendous obstacles to become journalists, writers, and novelists. They include National Book Award finalist and MacArthur Fellowship winner Edwidge Danticat, novelist Ernesto Quinonez, writer Veronica Chambers, and *New York Times* reporter Rachel Swarns. Hundreds more are working in law, business, and other careers. Many are teachers, principals, and youth workers, and several have started nonprofit youth programs themselves and work as mentors—helping another generation of young people develop their skills and find their voices.

Youth Communication is a nonprofit educational corporation. Contributions are gratefully accepted and are tax deductible to the fullest extent of the law.

To make a contribution, or for information about our publications and programs, including our catalog of over 100 books and curricula for hard-to-reach teens, see www.youthcomm.org.

About the Editors

Marie Glancy O'Shea is is the editor of *New Youth Connections*, Youth Communication's magazine by and for New York City teens. Before joining Youth Communication in 2008, she worked for several years in print, radio, and online journalism in Dublin, Ireland, and in New York. As an undergraduate she received a Harper's Magazine Scholarship from the Overseas Press Club Foundation. She has a BA in English from Williams College, an M Phil in Anglo-Irish literature from Trinity College Dublin, and an MS in journalism from Columbia University.

Keith Hefner co-founded Youth Communication in 1980 and has directed it ever since. He is the recipient of the Luther P. Jackson Education Award from the New York Association of Black Journalists and a MacArthur Fellowship. He was also a Revson Fellow at Columbia University.

Laura Longhine is the editorial director at Youth Communication. She edited *Represent*, Youth Communication's magazine by and for youth in foster care, for three years, and has written for a variety of publications. She has a BA in English from Tufts University and an MS in Journalism from Columbia University.

179

More Helpful Books
From Youth Communication

The Struggle to Be Strong: True Stories by Teens About Overcoming Tough Times. Foreword by Veronica Chambers. Help young people identify and build on their own strengths with 30 personal stories about resiliency. (Free Spirit)

Starting With "I": Personal Stories by Teenagers. "Who am I and who do I want to become?" Thirty-five stories examine this question through the lens of race, ethnicity, gender, sexuality, family, and more. Increase this book's value with the free Teacher's Guide, available from youthcomm.org. (Youth Communication)

Real Stories, Real Teens. Inspire teens to read and recognize their strengths with this collection of 26 true stories by teens. The young writers describe how they overcame significant challenges and stayed true to themselves. Also includes the first chapters from three novels in the Bluford Series. (Youth Communication)

The Courage to Be Yourself: True Stories by Teens About Cliques, Conflicts, and Overcoming Peer Pressure. In 26 first-person stories, teens write about their lives with searing honesty. These stories will inspire young readers to reflect on their own lives, work through their problems, and help them discover who they really are. (Free Spirit)

Out With It: Gay and Straight Teens Write About Homosexuality. Break stereotypes and provide support with this unflinching look at gay life from a teen's perspective. With a focus on urban youth, this book also includes several heterosexual teens' transformative experiences with gay peers. (Youth Communication)

 *Things Get Hectic: Teens Write About the Violence That Surrounds Them.* Violence is commonplace in many teens' lives, be it bullying, gangs, dating, or family relationships. Hear the experiences of victims, perpetrators, and witnesses through more than 50 real-world stories. (Youth Communication)

From Dropout to Achiever: Teens Write About School. Help teens overcome the challenges of graduating, which may involve overcoming family problems, bouncing back from a bad semester, or even dropping out for a time. These teens show how they achieve academic success. (Youth Communication)

 My Secret Addiction: Teens Write About Cutting. These true accounts of cutting, or self-mutilation, offer a window into the personal and family situations that lead to this secret habit, and show how teens can get the help they need. (Youth Communication)

Sticks and Stones: Teens Write About Bullying. Shed light on bullying, as told from the perspectives of the bully, the victim, and the witness. These stories show why bullying occurs, the harm it causes, and how it might be prevented. (Youth Communication)

 Boys to Men: Teens Write About Becoming a Man. The young men in this book write about confronting the challenges of growing up. Their honesty and courage make them role models for teens who are bombarded with contradictory messages about what it means to be a man. (Youth Communication)

Through Thick and Thin: Teens Write About Obesity, Eating Disorders, and Self Image. Help teens who struggle with obesity, eating disorders, and body weight issues. These stories show the pressures teens face when they are confronted by unrealistic standards for physical appearance, and how emotions can affect the way we eat. (Youth Communication)

To order these and other books, go to:
www.youthcomm.org
or call 212-279-0708 x115

CPSIA information can be obtained
at www.ICGtesting.com
Printed in the USA
BVHW01s0444200118
505641BV00006B/33/P

American ME

Teens Write About the Immigrant Experience

> *"Although I came here expecting our life to be as good or better than what we left behind, I know now that it is not easy to build a new life."*

Includes stories by teens from:

Albania	Ghana	Mexico
Bangladesh	Haiti	Philippines
Brazil	India	Peru
China	Iran	Russia
Dominican Republic	Iraq	Senegal
Ecuador	Korea	Venezuela
El Salvador	Malaysia	Yemen

ABOUT YOUTH COMMUNICATION: Founded in 1980, Youth Communication is a nonprofit youth journalism program that publishes teen stories in books, magazines, and on the Web. It has won awards from many organizations including:

- The Association of Educational Publishers
- The President's Council on the Arts and the Humanities
- Ment...
- Paren...
- Paren...

YOUTH
COMMUNICATION
True Stories by Teens